ANCESTORS IN THE ARCTIC

ANCESTORS IN THE ARCTIC:
A PHOTOGRAPHIC HISTORY OF DUNDEE WHALING

Malcolm Archibald

BLACK & WHITE PUBLISHING

First published 2013
by Black & White Publishing Ltd
29 Ocean Drive, Edinburgh EH6 6JL

1 3 5 7 9 10 8 6 4 2   13 14 15 16

ISBN: 978 1 84502 715 5

A CIP catalogue record for this book is available from the British Library.

Typeset by Creative Link, North Berwick
Printed and bound in Poland
www.hussarbooks.pl

This book is dedicated to the memory of all the
Dundee men who sailed to the whaling, and to the
women who waited for them

ACKNOWLEDGEMENTS

I would like to thank the following people and organisations
for their help in the research and writing of this book:
Leisure and Culture Dundee
Iain Flett and staff at Dundee Archives
The staff at the Central Library, Dundee
The people at Dundee University Archives

CONTENTS

FOREWORD

The collection of Dundee Art Galleries and Museums belongs to and has grown from the people of Dundee. Over 150 years it has become a wide and varied collection that includes archaeology, fine and applied art, natural history, social history and world cultures. In one way or another, whaling is reflected in almost all of these collections.

Many Dundonians have an awareness of the key role that whaling played in the history of the city, but for some it is still a hidden part of their heritage. Understanding such a hard, and at times brutal, industry from a twenty-first century viewpoint is not easy. Any form of trade that, by its very nature, is engaged in the culling of whales and seals on an industrial scale is difficult to explain in a world where such actions are widely condemned. The photographs contained in this book help to provide a context for Dundee whaling from a number of angles.

For the whaling company owners and the whaling men, it was simply their employment. Whales were commodities, and the products they spawned were demanded by the consumers of the eighteenth and nineteenth centuries. The photographs show the harsh realities of life for the whaling men, and indeed for the families who had to cope with the absence of their husbands and fathers for months at a time. They show the graceful ships that carried the crews and cargoes to and from such dangerous shores, and the incredible landscapes and people of the Arctic.

Above everything, the images demonstrate the central role whaling played in the working life of Dundee. Over one hundred vessels and thousands of men and women were involved in the industry in various ways, for over 160 years. It was all made possible by engineering and shipbuilding skills that were nurtured by the presence of the River Tay, an outlet to the world which made Dundee an outward-looking and internationally connected city.

Contained within the book is a selection of some of the best images from the museum collection. They were taken by early Dundee photographers who sailed with the whalers to the Arctic and made detailed photographic records of their voyages. Dundonians understand that collecting and preserving their material culture is core to preserving their identity. Acquisitions of items and stories relating to whaling continue to be made in order to strengthen the museum collection.

This book would not have been possible without the support of Museums Galleries Scotland, an organisation that actively encourages the development of collections. In 2008 Museums Galleries Scotland recognised the whaling collection to be of national significance, and funded The Dundee Whaling History Project, which aimed to comprehensively document the museum's collection and make links to related collections throughout Dundee. From that project, the need to produce a photographic publication was identified, and Museums Galleries Scotland have once again enabled access to the whaling collection by funding this publication.

The book itself is divided into five sections and is intended to flow like a voyage seen through the photographer's lens. The first photographic section shows whaling men at home, while the second highlights just a few of the ships that sailed from Dundee to hunt whales. The third is an evocative selection of whaling men working in the Arctic, and the fourth section reveals the strong bonds that the Dundee whalers developed with the local Inuit communities. The final section bids farewell to the industry.

On these pages you will find a fascinating overview of Dundee whaling. The text accompanying each photograph picks out key details and provides broad context, and will help the reader to study each image and draw their own informed conclusions. The photographs might act as a stimulus for discovering more about the whaling industry, or provide a gentle reminder that it is vital to continue to collect items relating to current industries in order to preserve them for future generations. More than anything, these evocative images have the power to bring a long gone industry, the people, the places, and the ships, back to life.

Fiona Sinclair
Museum Services Section Leader, Leisure and Culture Dundee

IMPORTANCE OF THE COLLECTION

The images in the whaling collection in Dundee Art Galleries and Museums can be used in a number of different ways. Each image is a free-frame of the period with its own points of interest that can be examined from a number of angles. With much of the collection digitised and available online, research is easier than ever before.

The images of the ships show details of the rigging, the hull shape, the equipment on board and the crew engaged in their various occupations. The images of the men show details of clothing that may be specific to place and conditions, as well as faces that could fit in to genealogical research. Work sequences are invaluable, as they show stage by stage exactly how whales were processed, from the initial towing to flensing – stripping the blubber from the whale – and making off the blubber. These images also show the often exhausted faces of the whaling men and remove any vestigial idea that there was glamour in an industry that was a combination of sheer work, danger and hardship.

If anything, the images of the whaling men at home with their wives and families are even more valuable. These photographs help dispel the image of whalers as a bunch of drunken brutes – 'a wild rough lot,' in the words of Christian Watt of Broadsea. Instead the family portraits reveal them as ordinary, respectable men who cared for their wives and families. There is no doubt that many whaling men were familiar with the pubs of Dock Street and the Overgate, and there were a few mutinies at sea, but over a period of over 160 years that is not too bad a record.

It is a major pity that photography was not more widespread in the early years of the century. Dundee Art Galleries and Museums do not hold any images of any of the Deuchars family, who played such a major part in Dundee whaling, while men such as William Adamson surely deserve to be depicted. However, what the museum does have is beyond price. The images of whaling captains Guy, Robertson, Milne, McKay and Adams show some of the most resolute and skilled mariners in the late Victorian and Edwardian age.

Lastly there are the splendid images of the Inuit, including a number that show the conditions in which they lived in the late nineteenth and early twentieth centuries. As the Inuit are increasingly assimilated into the twenty-first century, their traditional lifestyles are slipping into the past. These images are a reminder of when they were semi-nomadic hunter-gatherers who had adapted to survive and thrive in a very hostile environment. The faces that peer at the camera display bewilderment, joy, trust or simple pleasure. One major lesson is the obvious affection between the whaling men and the Inuit. When peoples from cultures so diametrically opposite can combine in friendship and even sexual relationships, then there is hope for the world.

THE DUNDEE WHALING INDUSTRY

In the early 1750s, Captain William Cheyne sailed the first known Dundee whaling ship to the Arctic. Her name was *Dundee* and she was the progenitor of an industry that survived in Dundee until 1914, long after whaling had faded from other British ports.

In the more than 160 years that Dundee ships scoured the Arctic there were innumerable setbacks, amazing triumphs, feats of incredible courage and days of terrible sadness. For year after year, Dundee sent ships north, normally in threes and fours but sometimes increasing to ten, twelve and as many as seventeen vessels, when the price of whale oil and baleen rose. The industry

provided employment to hundreds of people, from the fifty or so mariners who manned each vessel to the women who cleaned the filth from the whalebone and the wrights and artisans who built the ships. Add to that the grocers, blacksmiths, rope makers, sail makers, carters, butchers, wine merchants and whale oil dealers and the significance of the industry becomes clearer, and that is before the importance of whale oil to the jute industry is taken into consideration. Whaling was not created to provide excitement for daring men or an excuse to slaughter magnificent animals, but was a vital component of a thriving industrial town.

There were dynasties of Dundee whaling masters; the names

of Sturrock, Fairweather and Adams appear throughout the industry, while the Deuchars were ubiquitous, a family that was imbedded in whaling. There are also forgotten shipmasters such as Captain William Adamson, who fought the Dutch at the Battle of Camperdown, resisted a Royal Navy pressgang in his ship *Advice* and rescued the trapped Hull vessel *Swan* in 1836 by sawing through 3,000 feet of ice. His heroism is all but forgotten when the deeds of lesser men are proclaimed.

There were doubtless dynasties of harpooners, line managers and ordinary mariners as well, but history has obscured most of their names save for copperplate entries in surviving log books and bounty payments. Nevertheless, their faces stare out from the photographs in this book: men with features as familiar as our own as we see their descendants every day in the streets of Dundee and other east coast towns. They deserve to be better remembered. There is even less known of the wives of whaling men, but a few photographs remain, showing respectable, determined women who faced a tough life with courage typical of the age.

After decades of Dutch-dominated European whaling, in 1733 the British government decided to encourage their own whaling industry by offering a bounty for ships above a certain weight. There were few takers until the government doubled the bounty in 1750. Nearly overnight adventurers in Scotland and England invested their money in this hazardous industry. The new whaling companies had to obey stringent rules in order to qualify for the bounty. Ship owners, masters and mates all had to swear an oath that they intended to hunt for whales; they had to employ a number of raw hands, known as Greenmen, and they had to keep an accurate log that gave the precise location of any whales they saw. These rules may have been handicaps for the intended whaling adventurers, but they are a boon for modern historians. The custom and excise records and the logs that have survived are invaluable sources of information, as are the whaling journals of the ships' surgeons that the law also required the ships to carry.

In the early years many ships carried Dutch whaling specialists who taught their skills to the British mariners. These men also passed on some of the language, so Dutch whaling terms such as spectioneer (the head harpooner) became part of the common language in British Arctic ships. The vessels had flexible times for departure, but it in the days of sail it was usually March or April. They frequently called at Orkney or Shetland to complete their crew and hunted in the Greenland Sea between Greenland and Spitsbergen, or the Davis Strait between Greenland and Canada. They worked through the short Arctic summer and returned when the autumnal ice began to form or, if they had been fortunate, when their holds were crammed with reeking blubber.

Whales were hunted for two commodities: blubber and baleen. Blubber was boiled down for oil, which was used for street lamps until the advent of coal gas in the early nineteenth century and for domestic and factory lighting. In Dundee whale oil was also used for softening raw jute before it was processed into sacking and wagon covers and a hundred other things. Baleen was also known as whalebone and came from the jaw of the whale. It was an amazingly versatile material that could be turned into anything from chair backs to springs, but which was most used for corsets and in the hoops of crinoline skirts. When coal gas came into general use around the 1820s and then paraffin after 1859, the need for whale oil began a permanent slide, but Dundee's jute industry kept local demand high when other towns had withdrawn from the whaling trade.

The whaling men knew war as well as peace. In common with other British mariners they endured the various conflicts of the eighteenth century when French, Danish, Dutch and even American privateers and warships scoured the northern seas for prey, and a laden whaling ship made a tempting prize. In 1799 French privateers captured the Dundee whaling ship *Tay*, valued at a huge £6,000. There was also the press gang to dodge both onshore and off, for the Royal Navy had a nasty habit of cruising just off the coast to pounce on returning vessels and strip them of their crews. This happened to *Advice* in 1810. However, the Dundee whaling industry survived those hazards, as they survived the ice and storms of the north.

The end of the 1850s and beginning of the 1860s saw Dundee whaling enter its final and greatest era. In 1858 Dundee sent her first purpose-built steam whaling ships into the Arctic and the local shipbuilder, Alexander Stephen and Sons, proved expert in building what were probably the finest Arctic vessels the world had yet seen. Double planked, tripled at the bow, with seventy horsepower engines, retractable screws and internal bracing, Dundee vessels were sought by polar explorers from the United States to Australia. Many of these later vessels are illustrated in this book.

The whaling brought some terrible years for Dundee, as in 1837 when *Thomas* and *Active* were trapped in the Arctic ice and scores of men paid the ultimate price. *Active* returned as a floating morgue, full of dying men. There were weeping widows in the town then, and children without fathers. An estimated forty-six Dundee whaling ships were lost at sea, most beneath the ice of the Arctic, but *Horn* was swept ashore in St Andrews Bay, only a few miles from home. Add to that the constant drip of casualties, with men falling from spars, being swept overboard in stormy seas, dragged into the sea when a whale dived suddenly or suffering the agony of frostbite, and the true cost of the industry can be seen.

In the 1870s, Dundee vessels began to call regularly at St John's in Newfoundland and participate in the Newfoundland and Labrador sealing trade. Dundee entrepreneurs opened bases in St John's, and Newfoundland ship owners bought Dundee-built vessels in a display of inter-town co-operation that lasted decades. Dundee vessels probed deeper into the maritime fastnesses of Arctic Canada, opening up new areas in the desperate hunt for the diminishing resource of whales. In their quest, Dundee whaling men both befriended the local Inuit and made geographical discoveries that made them invaluable for the restless explorers who opened up the far north. Despite an abortive attempt to whale in the Antarctic, despite some of the best whaling masters and seamen in the world, and despite their superb ships, the Dundee whaling industry had not long to survive. Dundee Arctic whaling continued until 1914, when the crew of the last ship learned that war had begun with Germany and the world changed forever. It was the end of an era; it had been a good run for Dundee but the last years had been a struggle and Arctic whaling was dead.

It had been a rollercoaster of an industry with bad times and grieving widows, but there were good days as well when ships came home after a successful voyage, their holds stuffed full and even the whaleboats crammed with blubber. Then the pubs along Dock Street and the Overgate would be roaring with jovial whaling men as they celebrated their safe arrival. That is as good a place as any to leave this short introduction. The ships are berthed in Dundee, the crews are worshipping at the temple of Bacchus and the wives know their men are safe. Leave them in peace to enjoy their brief happiness.

THE MEN

Throughout the life of the Arctic whaling industry, Dundee produced a plethora of high-quality mariners, both as masters of the ships and the crews who sailed them into the north. Whaling was a branch of seamanship in which it was possible to rise through the ranks, and many of the best masters had learned their trade 'before the mast', which meant they had started in the forecastle with the ordinary seamen and learned each aspect of the trade by hard practical experience. Whaling masters bore the ultimate responsibility: they decided where to hunt, when to hunt and how to hunt. The shipmaster had to be an expert in whaling matters as well as in ship handling and ice navigation. Just as important, he had to have luck. For example, Captain Adams of *Arctic* always carried a penny of the reign of King George III for luck, and the men preferred a lucky captain in charge.

Beneath the master were the mates and the specialists: the oddly named spectioneers, the harpooners who attracted all the glamour; the boatsteerers who manoeuvred the whaleboats as close to the whales as possible; the line managers who ensured the whale lines ran smoothly; and the hard-working seamen who rowed the boats, kept the ship sailing and generally did everything that was necessary to make the industry a success. This section looks at some of the men who sailed the ships.

The passage of time has consigned most Dundee whaling masters to passing references in books, but some were well enough known in their day to have been photographed. Only one has his portrait in Dundee Art Galleries and Museums and that is Captain William Adams, Senior (1832–1890). W. Ferrier was the artist of this splendid oil painting of William Adams. It is a posthumous portrait, copied from a photograph. Adams is seated along with a map of the Davis Strait, the area in which he hunted whales.

William Adams was born in Dundee and was reputed to have sailed further north than any other Dundee whaling master. After some experience in other waters, Alexander Stephen employed Adams in the whaling industry in ships built at their own shipyard, *Arctic* and *Arctic II*. Adams retired in 1883, but he was not content living on shore and bought his own vessel, *Maud*. He commanded *Maud* on a number of voyages but took ill at sea and died shortly after he was brought ashore.

At the time of writing, the painting is displayed in The McManus: Dundee's Art Gallery and Museum alongside a selection of whaling objects.

In 1889 F. Livingstone-Learmonth took this photograph of Captain William Adams. He is in the crow's nest of the whaling ship *Maud*, presumably posing in a light-hearted manner. The photograph was taken while the crow's nest was resting on the deck of the ship. When the vessel was near to whale hunting grounds it would be hoisted to the upper section of the main mast. The crow's nest was usually a large barrel in which the master or another experienced man sat to look for whales, seals or anything that could endanger the vessel. The crow's nest in this photograph is equipped with a telescope on a slide that rotates 360 degrees. The Whitby whaler Captain William Scoresby has been credited with inventing the barrel crow's nest, but American whaling men also claimed that honour.

Captain Adams lived in West Ferry, beside Dundee. He made his first whaling voyage in 1850. He was master of the whaling vessel *Arctic* from 1869 to 1874, *Arctic II* from 1875 to 1883 and the owner and sometime master of *Maud* from 1884 until 1890. Adams was said to be the first man to take a whaling ship into Lancaster Sound, north of Baffin Island in Arctic Canada. He also helped search for survivors of the 1879 Tay Bridge Disaster. Dundee Art Galleries and Museums holds a number of objects related to him.

Dundee whaling shipmasters were some of the most highly skilled mariners anywhere. As well as having to know every facet of sailing a large vessel, whaling masters understood ice navigation and the management of crews that were reputedly by no means easy to handle. The best whaling masters could also be diplomats, dealing with the Inuit and the governors of the Danish settlements in Greenland.

There were rewards for such responsibilities. A whaling master of high reputation would be among the elite of the Dundee maritime community and would earn good money. In 1874 a Dundee whaling master earned a basic wage of £8 per month, plus £2 for every ton of whale oil produced and £7 for every ton of baleen. That same year the whaling ship *Ravenscraig* brought home over 200 tons of oil and six tons of bone, so the master would earn £442 over and above his basic wage.

This lantern slide shows a full-length portrait of a whaling shipmaster, probably Captain Guy. He is wearing a very respectable three-piece suit and a bowler hat. Captain Guy commanded a number of Dundee vessels, including *Polynia* and *Balaena*. He is mentioned in a Newfoundland folksong about *Polynia*:

Art Jackman set his canvas, Fairweather got up steam,
But Captain Guy, the daring boy, came plunging through the stream.
And Mullins in the Husky tried to beat the blooming lot,
But to beat the Old Polina was something he could not.

Dundee-born Captain Harry McKay is one of the greats of the whaling industry. It was Captain McKay who captained *Terra Nova* in the expedition to rescue the trapped Captain Scott in *Discovery* in 1904. He used explosives to free the ice-bound ship, but although that is the exploit for which he is best remembered, it was only one in an eventful life.

McKay was known as a handsome and charming man, and even Captain Scott of *Discovery*, who could be disparaging in his comments about whaling men, described him as 'excellent company for a depressed state of mind'. McKay was undoubtedly an expert Arctic seaman. The youngest whaling master in Dundee, he commanded *Aurora* from 1889 to 1893, which was the year in which he located the wreck of *Ripple*, the vessel of the Swedish Arctic explorers Bjorling and Kalstenius. The Swedish Anthropological and Geographical Society awarded McKay a medal for his endeavours. In 1894 and 1897 he was master of *Terra Nova*, and in 1898 he took the Coats family of Paisley on an Arctic cruise in their yacht *Blencathra*. In 1900 he was master of *Esquimaux*, from which ship he transferred to *Terra Nova* once more. After his skill in rescuing *Discovery* McKay became master of *Diana* from 1905 to 1909. When not voyaging around the Arctic, Harry McKay found time to marry and raise four children.

This black and white photograph by W. Ferrier shows Captain McKay wearing a nautical cap complete with the badge of the Royal Tay Yacht Club.

As the nineteenth century closed, the special qualities of Dundee whaling shipmasters began to be recognised. In an age of polar exploration, many were recruited for their expertise in Arctic seamanship. One such was Captain Thomas Robertson.

According to Basil Lubbock in his book *Arctic Whalers*, Captain Robertson was known as 'Coffee Tam' for his teetotal propensities. He is perhaps better known for having commanded *Active* in the 1892 Dundee Antarctic Expedition. The scientist William Bruce was so impressed with Robertson's qualities that he asked him to take charge of *Scotia* in the Scottish National Antarctic Expedition of 1902. This expedition scientifically explored the Weddell Sea (named after the Scottish sealer James Weddell), but the British government refused to award any polar medals. The government perhaps saw a successful and purely Scottish expedition as a dangerous rival to their own efforts. However, the Royal Scottish Geographical Society awarded Robertson a silver medal. After an iceberg sank the passenger liner *Titanic* in 1912, Captain Robertson was requested to command *Scotia* on ice patrols in the North Atlantic. In between these exciting endeavours, he also had time to be a successful whaling shipmaster.

Alexander Roger took this lantern slide, which shows Robertson on the bridge of *Active* in 1894, a year after his first return from the Antarctic.

This photograph shows Captain William Fraser Milne standing on the deck of a Dundee whaling ship. Although only five foot high, Captain Milne commanded great respect from his crew, his peers and an impressive list of Arctic explorers.

As well as an expert on the Inuit, Captain Milne was one of Dundee's leading whaling masters and the Commodore of the Dundee whaling fleet. At various times he commanded *Esquimaux, Eclipse, Diana, Albert* and *Maud*. In 1902, when the Norwegian Roald Amundsen planned to navigate a vessel through the North West Passage from the Davis Straits to the Pacific Ocean, he turned to Milne for help. Milne advised Amundsen on the best route to take. Amundsen followed Milne's route through Lancaster Sound, Barrow Strait and Peel Sound into Franklin Strait and became the first man to navigate the passage. Augmenting his advice, Milne also transported stores to Amundsen's supply depot past Cape York. It is not surprising that King Haakon of Norway made Milne a Knight of the Second Class of the Order of St Olaf. He was probably the only Dundee whaling master to be so honoured.

Milne was also a friend of other Arctic explorers including Dr Nansen, Lieutenant Greely and Lieutenant Peary. He donated a reindeer to Dundee Museum, rescued the crew of the shipwrecked Newfoundland vessel *Eagle* and studied the habits of the whale, while fathering ten children in his fifty-five-year-long marriage. All in all, William Milne was an outstanding example of a Dundee whaling master.

Many Dundee whaling masters were highly respected by the men who sailed with them. Captain William Milne was one of them. Captain Milne was born in Peterhead but was master of Dundee vessels from 1883 until 1910. He is probably best remembered for his fifteen-year command of *Eclipse*, although he was also involved in

the speculative, but ultimately abortive, Gold Exploration Syndicate of Peterhead.

In this image Captain Milne is seated on the deck of *Eclipse*. He is in the centre of the picture with a neat beard and is wearing a bowler hat. Eleven of his crew are artistically posed around him. To judge by their clothing, the photograph was taken somewhere at the beginning of the twentieth century. Photographs of any shipmaster of that period in the company of his crew are comparatively rare, so this picture might indicate that Captain Milne had a special bond with his men. The gentleman seated on the captain's left is the ship's carpenter, one of the specialists that whaling ships needed to carry.

This photograph shows one of the specialists that whaling ships carried on board. These men were not always strictly seamen, although they played a vital part in every voyage; they included the sail maker, blacksmith and carpenter.

The carpenter was responsible for all the woodwork on board the ship – and there was a lot of it. He had the task of ensuring the hull remained watertight and the masts and spars were in good condition, while the whaleboats were seaworthy. If the ship or the whaleboats were damaged by ice, the carpenter had to repair them. Some carpenters were also involved in securing the anchor and in loading fresh water. If he had time from his often onerous duties in a wooden ship working in harsh conditions, the carpenter might also have had a second occupation. For instance, James Alexander, the carpenter of the Dundee whaling ship *Jan Mayen* in 1881, was both carpenter and harpooner. He would have worked a full apprenticeship to gain the necessary carpentering skills and qualifications to work and in 1874 earned £3 ten shillings a month, plus oil and bone money.

This sepia print shows William Scott, the carpenter of *Narwhal* around 1880. He is wearing a very formal uniform and cap that would certainly be out of place on board a whaling ship.

James McIntosh was a bit of a legend in Dundee. He was born in Australia of a Dundee father, but returned to Scotland and became a seaman. His first voyage was to the Baltic at the age of fourteen, but he soon transferred to the whaling trade.

In 1884, aged twenty-eight, he sailed on *Chieftain*, a three-masted schooner. He was out in a whaleboat in the Greenland Sea, hunting for bottle-nosed whales, or 'botleys' as they were termed, when a mist descended. The boat lost contact with *Chieftain*. McIntosh took charge of the steering oar in the stern but could

only watch as the other members of the boat died of hunger and exposure. Some drank seawater and went mad. Days later McIntosh was rescued, but he was so badly frostbitten that he had to be cut free of the boat and a surgeon had to amputate both legs below the knee.

McIntosh never went to sea again but became a level-crossing attendant at Broughty Ferry. He became something of a local celebrity and there is a play written about him. McIntosh was a married man and had six sons and four daughters. This photograph shows him with Helen Campbell Stuart, his wife, around 1900.

Christian Watt of Broadsea called them a 'wild, rough lot' and the Reverend John Mill of Sandwick, Shetland, said they were 'curs'd ruffians', Sir Walter Scott thought them 'drunken, riotous sailors' and thought that 'between whisky and frolic the Greenland sailor will certainly burn the little town of Lerwick'. Yet although whaling men were frequently seen as violent and troublesome, most of them were ordinary married men with a family. Whaling to them was only a job to raise money to pay the bills and feed their wife and children.

Alexander Watt of 41 Arbroath Road in Dundee took this sepia photograph that shows the whaling man Nicholas White, his wife Margaret and their family around 1890. All are very respectably dressed, and the parents appear attached to their children. Margaret has a fine long dress with a vertical stripe, while her hair is pulled back with a centre parting in the fashion of the time. Nicholas is wearing a suit and a tie and sports the beard worn by many whaling men.

Nicholas White was born in Cork in 1853. He served on the whaling ship *Balaena* as a harpooner and steward. He married Margaret and settled at 1 Park Avenue, Dundee, where they raised their family. Margaret would have been very concerned in 1895 when *Balaena* was believed missing in the Arctic, but the ship and all her crew turned up safe and well.

By the beginning of the twentieth century, Dundee's polar expertise was in demand. Dundee-built ships and Dundee seamen were much sought after by the turn-of-the-century explorers who were pushing back the frontiers with every expedition.

One of the most famous of all the Antarctic explorers was Captain Robert Falcon Scott, who in 1901 led the *Discovery* expedition towards the South Pole. His expedition was largely composed of Royal Naval personnel with no Arctic or Antarctic experience, and soon came to grief. *Discovery* became trapped in the Antarctic ice. Two ships, *Morning* and *Terra Nova*, were despatched to relieve the stranded explorers with the Dundee whaling master Captain Harry McKay commanding *Terra Nova*. As mentioned earlier, the rescue expedition was a success, with *Discovery* and her crew being freed by explosives.

This photograph shows the officers and crew of *Terra Nova* before they sailed south to rescue Captain Scott. The officers are lined up on the quarterdeck, wearing naval uniforms and flat caps, with Captain Harry McKay prominent in the left centre. In front of the officers and slightly lower down are the crew. All are wearing uniforms, some the dark blue of the Royal Navy, others white, and those that wear hats have the name *Terra Nova* on them. This expedition showed the real skill and expertise of Dundee whaling masters and men as they sailed to rescue a commander of the Royal Navy who had got himself into difficulties in an environment unfamiliar to him, but in which the Dundee men excelled.

Overall, the sailors of the Dundee whaling ships were amongst the hardiest masters and mariners afloat, but they were also family men with wives and families who depended on the pay packets they brought home. Every spring they would sail north to the Arctic seas, but to do so they needed ships that were every bit as sturdy as they were themselves. The next section looks at these whaling vessels.

SECTION TWO

THE SHIPS

ithout the ships there would have been no whaling industry. The ships carried the men to the Arctic and carried the blubber and baleen back to Dundee. As they operated in some of the toughest conditions imaginable, they had to be strongly constructed. Their hulls were double planked, which meant they had twice the thickness of other vessels, while the bows were treble planked, with internal beams for further strength.

Whaling vessels were also known as 'Greenlandmen' or, more derogatively, as 'blubber boats'. At the beginning of the nineteenth century most Dundee whaling vessels were around 100 feet

(about thirty metres) long, but the size increased as the years rolled past. The major breakthrough occurred with the advent of steam-powered whaling ships in 1858. From that date Dundee-built and Dundee-owned ships dominated Arctic whaling. However, steam did have disadvantages as well, with coal taking up valuable cargo space and having to be purchased, and specialist engineers hired for the engines. As compensation, the power of their engines enabled steam vessels to penetrate further into the ice than sailing vessels ever could.

This section includes images of some of the most important vessels that sailed from Dundee in the later nineteenth century,

including some technical specifications, a brief history of the vessel and details, if known, of the actual photograph. Maritime historians as well as native Dundonians and those with an ancestral whaling collection may find this section interesting.

In the nineteenth century Dundee was a major port with shipping links that extended from India to Russia and the Mediterranean to Arctic Canada. There were four main docks: Victoria, King William IV, Camperdown and, the smallest of them all, Earl Grey. This last dock was opened in 1834 and named after the 2nd Earl Grey, who was Prime Minister at the time of the Great Reform Act that increased the franchise. Reform Street in Dundee was named after that seminal incident in British politics.

Earl Grey Dock was often home to ships of the Dundee whaling fleet. In this evocative lantern slide two whaling ships are berthed in the calm waters of the dock. Both are riding high, so it is likely that they are not carrying a cargo. They are either about to sail north or have not long returned.

This print shows two ships of the Dundee fleet around 1906. The closest vessel is *Windward*, which sailed from Dundee from 1904 until 1907, while the second vessel is *Morning*, which was part of the Dundee fleet from 1905 until 1914.

Windward was a Peterhead-built vessel, while *Morning* was built in Norway, but both participated in the Dundee whaling industry. The whaling ships could berth in Earl Grey or Victoria Dock in Dundee. By this period they would often sail on two voyages a year; they would leave in February for a short voyage to the sealing grounds of the Greenland Sea around Spitsbergen or Jan Mayen Land, followed by a return to Dundee to land their catch. Once the ships were re-equipped, and sometimes with some changes in personnel, they sailed again on the much longer voyage to the whaling grounds of the Davis Strait, Hudson Strait or Hudson Bay.

Morning had an exciting career. She was involved in the rescue of Captain Scott's *Discovery* in 1904, and while part of the Dundee fleet she also rescued the crew of *Windward* when that vessel foundered in 1907. Her more usual occupation, however, was in catching whales. In 1909 she worked in the Greenland Sea and the Davis Strait, catching whales, white whales, walruses and bears.

Many of the vessels in Dundee's whaling fleet had interesting careers. One such was the whaling ship *Scotia*. Built in Norway in 1872, *Scotia* was bought by William Bruce in 1902 for the Scottish National Antarctic Expedition of 1902–1904. The Dundee whaling master, Captain Thomas Robertson, commanded her during this expedition. Although she was locked in the ice for eight months in Scotia Bay, she returned safely to Scotland. She joined the Dundee whaling fleet in 1905, the same year that she rescued the crew of a Norwegian sealing ship who had been adrift for seventeen days. In 1913, after the loss of *Titanic,* and still with Robertson in command, *Scotia* became an ice patrol vessel. Her final years were less glorious; she was sold to the Hudson Bay Company and during the First World War she was chartered to the French government as a munitions ship. *Scotia* was lost in the Bristol Channel in 1916.

This photograph shows *Scotia* in a quiet Dundee dock. She is riding high in the water and is far too spick and span to have returned from an Arctic voyage, so presumably was being prepared to sail north. In common with many Dundee whaling ships of the period, she is a wooden-built auxiliary screw barque.

In the early twentieth century Dundee was the last surviving British port to actively pursue the Arctic whaling trade. Around 1905, the approximate date this photograph was taken, Dundee had eight vessels involved in whaling. Two of these vessels are pictured in Dundee Docks. *Balaena* is stern on and nearer the camera, with *Windward* bow on to the camera and to the right.

Balaena was a Norwegian-built vessel that sailed in the Dundee fleet from 1891 until Dundee whaling ended in 1914. She was part of the Dundee Antarctic Expedition of 1892, and in 1901 her master, Captain Robertson, was fined for having smuggled tobacco in his cabin. *Windward* was built in Peterhead and was only in the Dundee fleet from 1904 until 1907. That year she was wrecked on Carey Island in Hudson Bay in Canada. As so often happened with Arctic whaling ships, the crew was all rescued. In 1904 she had a variety of owners in Dundee, including a shipmaster, a coppersmith, an oil merchant and a cooper. At that period it was common for people to buy a share or two in a ship as an investment.

Figureheads were quite controversial in whaling ships, as some seamen suggested that they collected ice that might endanger the ship. There is a story that the crew of the Hull whaling ship *Truelove* believed her ice-coated figurehead pulled her down by the bows, so they hacked it off. Nevertheless, a number of Dundee whaling ships were so decorated. Figureheads are as old as ships, with very early ships in the Mediterranean being launched over a human sacrifice and the head of the unlucky man placed on the prow of the ship to prove to the sea god that the blood sacrifice had been made. Even as late as the nineteenth century some superstitious seamen believed that the figurehead carried the luck of the ship. They were maintained in perfect condition, for any damage to the figurehead would lessen the luck of the ship and correspondingly lower the morale of the crew.

This is *Active* in Dundee Dock around 1894. The male figurehead of a man in the dress of an early nineteenth-century seaman is very visible. It was comparatively unusual to have a figurehead of a man, as some seamen believed that a female, particularly a bare-breasted female, had the power to calm storms.

Taken around 1906, this powerful shot shows the Dundee whaling fleet leaving port. This time was very emotional for both the whaling crews and for the families they left behind. Although whaling men might not be perceived as the most demonstrative of people, some of the comments made as they left port could be illuminating. John Wanless, the young surgeon of *Thomas* in 1834, wrote of 'my throbbing heart on seeing my town sink in the horizon'. W. Burn Murdoch, an artist who accompanied the 1892 Dundee Antarctic Expedition, wrote of men bidding 'goodbye to their wives and children' and faces 'wet with tears'.

The women and children would know that their men would be gone for months, and there was always a possibility some might not return. It was no wonder that a minister gave a service before the ships sailed, while some of the more superstitious of the women left tokens to bring luck in various parts of the ship. Other seamen preferred to spend their last hours on shore in a drunken binge.

The vessel closest to the camera might be *Active*, a square-sterned barque that was part of the Dundee fleet from 1874 to 1916. She is under steam power with all her sails furled and at her main mast she wears the Kinnes House flag of a star. At that time Robert Kinnes was arguably the most important man in British whaling.

Windward was one of the later Dundee whaling vessels. As previously mentioned, she was built in Peterhead and was part of the Dundee fleet from 1904 until 1907, so this lantern slide of her leaving Dundee docks can be accurately dated to that period. Unusually for Dundee whaling ships, she was clinker-built, which meant her hull planks overlapped each other rather than meeting end-to-end as was more normal at the time. *Windward* had a thirty-five horsepower engine as well as her sails but was not a very effective whale catcher, managing to bring home only one white and three black whales in her time in Dundee.

As always when a whaling vessel departed Dundee for the Arctic, a crowd gathered to see her off. Many of the people watching would be related to the men on board and they would hope for a successful voyage and a safe return home. The wives would be alone for months at a time, and although they would be able to draw a portion of their husband's pay, they would need to work to make enough money to survive until their husbands returned. It was not an easy life for a whaling man's wife and family.

This photograph shows the stern view of a whaling ship sailing into the River Tay from Dundee. She is wearing flags from every mast, including the Kinnes House flag of a star, which is at her mizzen. Robert Kinnes was one of the most important British whaling-ship owners of the late nineteenth and early twentieth centuries.

This ship is possibly about to embark on her whaling or sealing voyage. There is a large crowd of men in the stern, perhaps toasting the health of the forthcoming trip. Many contemporary observers wrote about the beginning of these voyages, with Admiral Seymour saying the crew of the Dundee whaling ship *Mazinthien* were not 'over sober' when they sailed, and the *Dundee Directory* of 1875 commenting that 'incidents of mingled excitement and amusement frequently arise'. Captain Markham, who sailed on *Arctic* in the early 1870s, wrote that the 'scene on board an outward-bound whaler on the eve of departure has been described to be as both filthy and disgusting'. However, Markham also stated that '*Arctic*'s Crew are an exception', with Captain Adams calling them a 'good and sober crowd'.

From the Tay, the whaling vessel would call at Shetland for extra hands and coal before embarking for the perils of the Arctic.

This picture captures some of the atmosphere of whaling in the days of steam and sail. The photograph was taken from the deck of an unknown vessel and shows the Dundee whaling ship *Active* stern on and moving under sail power in an exceptionally calm sea. Although sea-going steamships had been known since the voyage of *Comet* in 1812, Dundee whaling vessels were among the many ships that still relied partly or wholly on sail power. Perhaps that was because the wind was a free source of energy, while coal was bulky and expensive.

Active was built in Peterhead in 1852 and sailed from Dundee from 1874 until the end of Dundee Arctic whaling in 1914. She was originally a purely sail-powered vessel, but Hall Russell of Aberdeen added engines around 1870. Gourlays of Dundee compounded the engines in 1873. At 117 feet long she was smaller than the average whaling ship of her period, but her lifespan of over sixty years proved her a tough and durable vessel.

Towards the end of the nineteenth century some photographers travelled on Dundee whaling ships to capture the essence of the industry, both the hard work and the romantic image of life in the Arctic.

In the final decades of the nineteenth century Dundee was Europe's leading Arctic whaling port. At its peak, the port sent up to seventeen ships annually to the whaling grounds of the Greenland Sea and Davis Strait.

This photograph shows the Dundee whaling ship *Eclipse*. Built in Aberdeen in 1867, *Eclipse* was part of the Dundee fleet from 1892 until 1909. She had an interesting career while in Dundee ownership, striking rocks near Disko Island in the Davis Strait in 1902 and helping rescue the crew of *Nova Zembla* when that vessel was wrecked the same year.

When whaling ships were in the Arctic they often moored to ice floes when the men were out sealing or taking in fresh water from the ice. In this picture she is moored while the crew flense a small whale that is on her port side. Whale catches had decreased substantially by this period and a whale of any size was fair game.

Eclipse has her sails furled but the wisp of smoke from her funnel shows that she would not take long to have her steam up and be ready to sail away. In the Arctic it was best to always be prepared, as a sudden change in the weather could bring danger from the ice. Despite their especially strong hulls, over forty Dundee whaling ships were lost in the Arctic.

Although working in the Arctic posed many problems for the whaling men, there were also some advantages. Unless the ship was trapped in the ice for a very long period, the health of the crew was usually good, as there were no exotic diseases such as those that could occur on voyages to tropical destinations. It was also possible to replenish the fresh water, which is what is happening to the Dundee whaling ship *Eclipse* in this photograph. *Eclipse* is moored to pack ice, with her sails furled. There is some work being done to her jib sail at her bowsprit, while a number of men are on the ice preparing to take on ice for water. There is also a man in the crow's nest, probably watching for whales or a sudden alteration of the weather. There is a dog on the ice. In common with other seamen, whaling men sometimes had pets on board.

Eclipse was a lovely vessel with black-painted topsides and a white poop and bulwarks and, as can be seen in the photograph, her lower foremast and main mast were also painted white. Her mizzen was black, presumably because it would have been hard to keep white with her funnel emitting smuts and smoke, and was partly sheathed in copper to ensure protection from the heat.

Over the 160-plus years of her involvement in Arctic whaling, Dundee had around a hundred whaling or sealing vessels. Some are still remembered while others are forgotten by all but a few maritime specialists.

One vessel of the early twentieth century was the Norwegian-built *Morning*. She was over 440 tons gross and was a two-decked single-screw steam vessel with three masts. In this lantern slide she has sails set on her fore and main mast and is making good speed running before the wind on a lively sea. Her crow's nest is unmanned, which suggests that she was not near whaling grounds at the time. Svend Foyn, the Norwegian who improved

the whaling gun, designed *Morning* and the British government purchased her in 1902. She accompanied *Terra Nova* in the *Discovery* Relief Expedition of that year.

Captain Adams commanded *Morning* when she sailed from Dundee. This photograph might have been taken in 1906 when the photographer and lecturer Sandon Perkins sailed on her to the Davis Strait. The following year *Morning* was involved in the rescue of the crew of the wrecked Dundee whaling ship *Windward*. In common with so many other Dundee whaling ships, she was lost during the First World War.

ASSEMBLY ROOMS

Great Malvern

SATURDAY,

28th MARCH 1908

AT 3 AND 8 O'CLOCK.

Mr M. T. STEVENS has pleasure in announcing an ILLUSTRATED LECTURE by

SANDON PERKINS

The well=Known Traveller and Explorer, entitled—

"'MIDST ARCTIC SNOWS"

Giving an Account of his recent voyage to the Polar Regions on the "Morning."

ANIMATED PICTURES AND PHOTOGRAPHS taken by Mr Sandon Perkins will be exhibited.

Tour Direction—
BARING BROS.

Doors open at 2.30 and 7.30.   Carriages at 4.30 and 9.30.

AFTERNOON - Reserved and Numbered Seats, 3s. ; Second Seats, 2s. ; Third Seats, 1s.
EVENING - -   Do.   do.   2s. ;   Do.   1s. ;   Do.   6d.

Special Arrangements for Schools.   PLAN AND TICKETS AT THE BOX OFFICE, CHURCH ST.

Throughout the nineteenth century, tales of exploration were popular with the British public. Explorers such as David Livingstone or John Ross came home from the far corners of the world and lectured to packed audiences about the strange things they had seen and people they had met. These events were public entertainment as well as education. By the beginning of the twentieth century explorers and adventurers had recognised the value of Dundee whaling men in transporting them to the far corners of the Arctic.

Sandon Perkins was one such adventurer who was well known in his day, although history seems to have largely forgotten him now. He travelled to the Arctic in the Dundee whaling ship *Morning* in 1906, taking photographs, experiencing the harsh conditions and meeting the Inuit. Perkins used his travels to give lecture tours all across the globe as well as in the UK. This leaflet advertises his lecture 'Midst Arctic Snows', which was presented at the Assembly Rooms in Great Malvern on Saturday, 28 March 1908. The illustration shows a bearded and tough-looking Perkins, which is doubtless the image he intended to portray.

Whaling vessels usually hunted on the same grounds and were often in close proximity to one another. The shipmasters often crossed from one vessel to another to exchange news or just to pass a pleasant few hours together, while the men could play football on the ice. On many occasions, when the ice sank a whaling ship the crew would cross to a nearby ship. Such events were quite common and explained the number of ships that sank with only minimal casualties.

This lantern slide shows two Dundee vessels, *Nova Zembla* and *Eclipse*, anchored close together in the Arctic. Both vessels have their sails furled but their crow's nests hoisted. *Nova Zembla* was German-built but the Dundee Polar Fishing Company bought her in 1875. Her original name was *Novaya Semblaya*. She was a fairly successful vessel at both whaling and sealing until she was abandoned in Dexterity Fjord on the east coast of Baffin Island in Canada in 1902. In common with some other Dundee whaling vessels, she had a fairly uneventful career until she was lost, with no major adventures, which is possibly why she is barely remembered now.

By the early eighteenth century, European whaling ships were hunting in the Davis Strait, the stretch of ice and water between Greenland and the eastern coast of Canada. It was common practice for them to round Cape Farewell at the southern tip of Greenland and sail to the island of Disko. They would rendezvous there and make ready for the hazardous crossing of Melville Bay to the 'West Water', the whaling grounds on the opposite side of the strait.

Sometimes the journey across the Bay would end in disaster. In 1830 nineteen British whaling ships were lost when a passage in the ice closed on them. Around 1,000 men were stranded on the ice. Rather than despair, they removed the rum stores from the stricken ships and had a party. This incident has been remembered as the Baffin Fair.

This lantern slide shows the Dundee whaling ship *Eclipse* moored off Disko Island. The photograph was taken at the turn of the nineteenth and twentieth centuries when there were far fewer whaling ships operating and whales were scarce in this area. *Eclipse* was an auxiliary steam-powered vessel that was in the Dundee fleet from 1892 until 1909.

By the latter decades of the nineteenth century, the ships of the Dundee whaling fleet were built to a similar style. They were double-hulled with heavily reinforced bows and were three-masted with auxiliary steam engines. Many had been built by Alexander Stephen of Marine Parade and they were probably the best Arctic vessels in the world.

One of these ships was *Esquimaux,* pictured here in calm water at the edge of the Arctic ice. She was built in 1865 and at 660 tons gross was one of the larger whaling vessels of her period. Built entirely of wood, she was just less than 160 feet long, and a seventy horsepower engine was added in 1866. After a maiden voyage to Archangel, she successfully sailed with the Dundee whaling fleet until 1898 with the usual quota of incidents. In 1895 she ran aground at Disko and two years later she had forty-three stowaways in a crew of 375 while at the Greenland sealing. Most of these men joined at St John's Newfoundland. In 1898 she was sold to Liverpool owners. Refitted in Dundee as a pleasure yacht in 1899, the following year she became an exploration ship. Renamed *America*, she was lost in the Arctic in 1903.

By the nineteenth century Dundee whaling ships were as experienced at hunting in the Davis Strait between Greenland and Canada as their European counterparts. They often rendezvoused at the island of Disko on the west coast of Greenland where the Danes had established small villages. The early whaling men had a rhyme that said:

With Riff Koll Hill and Disko dipping
There you'll see the whale fish skipping

At the beginning of the nineteenth century over a hundred whaling ships could rendezvous there, waiting for the ice to melt so they could cross Melville Bay. However by the latter years of the century there were few whales in the vicinity of Disko and whaling ships were less likely to call there before heading west to the whaling grounds of Melville Bay.

This photograph shows the Dundee ship *Balaena* lying near the mountains of Disko. The men working on the ice can be plainly seen, as can the whaleboats hanging in the davits ready to be launched. *Balaena* was a Norwegian-built ship that was in the Dundee whaling fleet from 1890 until she was sold to Liverpool owners in 1917. This photograph was taken around the turn of the nineteenth and twentieth centuries.

Launched at Alexander Stephen's Marine Parade yard in 1884, *Terra Nova* was the last Dundee-built whaling ship and arguably the best. With her registered tonnage at 450, she was a fairly large vessel for a whaling ship. In her first whaling and sealing voyage to Newfoundland, *Terra Nova* accounted for over 21,000 seals, plus eight whales, which was accounted a successful voyage. She was powerful for her time but was hardly fuel efficient by today's standards, burning fourteen tons of coal in twenty-four hours if sailing at full speed.

As well as a whaling vessel, *Terra Nova* was used for exploration. Captain Harry McKay of Dundee sailed her to rescue Captain Scott of *Discovery* in 1903 and she was also involved in the rescue of an American expedition to Franz Joseph Land in 1905. *Terra Nova* returned to the Antarctic in 1910 when Scott sailed her on his fatal South Pole adventure.

In this photograph, *Terra Nova* is riding light on the water, with

the Plimsoll mark clearly visible on her black-painted hull. She is barque rigged and the details of her rigging can clearly be seen. Dundee Art Galleries and Museums hold a splendid model of this historic vessel.

Alexander Rodger was a museum assistant at Dundee University and made two trips north with whaling ships to collect Arctic specimens. This photograph is from his voyage in *Active* in 1894. It shows *Active* near Spitsbergen in pack ice. Her barque rig is plainly visible, as are the whaleboats hanging from davits and a man in the crow's nest, either searching the ice for seals or looking for a clear patch of water to guide the ship toward. It is possible the sails were set purely for the photograph, as the men on board all appear to be looking towards the camera and *Active* does not seem to be making any progress! This voyage was not a success, as Captain Brown fell sick and *Active* had to return home to Dundee after capturing only two whales. However, the presence of Rodger on board ensured that there was a fine photographic record of Arctic whaling.

Active had a long life for an Arctic whaler and was one of the last working Dundee whaling ships. She was built in Peterhead in 1852, joined the Dundee whaling fleet in 1874 and took part in the Dundee Antarctic Whaling Expedition of 1892–93. On this voyage Captain Thomas Robertson discovered and named Dundee Island and one of *Active's* crew harpooned a blue whale. However, the animal was far too powerful to be caught and it towed *Active* astern for some time before escaping. *Active's* engines only generated forty horsepower: not enough to stop a full-grown blue whale. The following year *Active* was back in Greenland waters, but she also operated in Hudson Bay. She was trapped in pack ice in the autumn of 1879 when the main sea-cock froze and the ship had to stop to effect repairs. She survived until 1916.

A number of well-known whaling masters commanded *Active*, including James Fairweather, who said of her: 'She was my first command and I was very proud of her . . . I thought her a thing of beauty.'

Getting stuck in the ice was a major danger for whaling vessels. Sailing ships would try to break through by either 'rolling' the ship, which meant having the crew run from side to side to create a rocking motion, or by the crude method of raising a whaleboat over the bow and dropping it on the ice to crack it. The later steam vessels were more powerful and could sometimes muscle their way through. The vessels all had specially strengthened bows with internal braces and external plating.

However, there were times when the ice was too thick for even a steam engine and more drastic measures were required. The whaling master could use gunpowder to blast a passage in the ice, or to weaken the ice so the ship could break through. In 1904 Captain McKay of the Dundee ship *Terra Nova* used gunpowder when he helped free Captain Scott's *Discovery*, when the latter was trapped in the ice during the British Antarctic Expedition.

This picture might be of the Dundee whaling ship *Maud*, a Whitby-built vessel that sailed from Dundee from 1884 until she was wrecked in the Davis Strait in 1892. Originally a sail-powered vessel, she was converted to steam in Dundee. In this picture she is moored to the ice and might be in the process of blasting a channel.

Arctic whaling could be quite a convivial activity. Whenever two whaling ships met, the masters could pay a social call on each other and exchange news about whale activity and how successful their hunting had been so far. The crew could also pay visits, crossing the ice to the neighbouring ship.

This lantern slide shows two Dundee whaling ships anchored to an ice floe somewhere in the Arctic. Both vessels are wearing the Union flag on their mizzen and are barque rigged – the mizzen mast is rigged for fore-and-aft sails rather than square sails. The nearest vessel has the name *Nova Zembla* on her bow and there are a number of men visible on her bowsprit, possibly watching the photographer at work.

Built in 1873, *Nova Zembla* was a barque-rigged steamer with an engine of fifty-eight horsepower, which made her slightly underpowered by the standards of other Dundee vessels. The Dundee Polar Fishing Company brought her from Germany, but, as mentioned above, in 1902 she was abandoned and lost in Dexterity Fjord in Arctic Canada. Dundee owners bought a number of German-built vessels late in the nineteenth century. One, *Spitzbergen*, sank before she reached Dundee.

This photograph shows the Dundee whaling ship *Maud*. As already mentioned, this vessel was built at Whitby in 1865. Whitby had been a whaling port from 1753 until 1837. *Maud* was a sailing vessel when Captain William Adams bought her in 1884, but two years later he converted her to steam, with engines by Whyte and Cooper of Dundee. This photograph was taken some time after her conversion in 1886 and before 1892, when she was wrecked in Coutts Inlet in the Davis Strait. This photograph shows *Maud* negotiating pack ice; she is under sail and heeling slightly, with her whaleboats hanging on their davits.

Whaling ships such as *Maud* were specially strengthened to work in such conditions. Their hulls were 'doubled', which meant they had an extra layer of planking, and they were 'trebled' at the bows. There were also internal supports to help the vessels withstand the pressure of the ice.

As soon as a whaling ship approached the whaling grounds, the master ordered the whaleboats checked and onto the davits, ready to be launched the instant a whale was sighted. Often there would be one boat sitting in the sea, 'on bran' as it was termed. A streak of dark water is visible astern of *Maud* in this photograph, so it appears she has just entered the ice.

Viewing any ship from the outside only gives a very small part of the story. Before she was built, a team of designers and specialists would examine every function the vessel was expected to perform and would draw up plans that would be converted first into a scale model of the vessel and then into the ship.

The interior of the vessel was as important as the exterior, with every square inch measured and accounted for so the crew, the cargo, the stores and the coal were all fitted in. This scale drawing of *Terra Nova* was printed by Harrison and Sons of London. It shows the hull and cross section with a scale of one-eighth of an inch to a foot, or 1:96. The details of the interior of this vessel can be seen, giving an idea of how little space the crew enjoyed when they were sailing her in some of the most hostile waters in the world. It is perhaps no wonder that seamen were often afflicted with tuberculosis when they were allowed so little breathing space in the forecastle where they spent their off-duty hours.

TERRA NOVA.

Scale, $\frac{1}{8}$" – 1'.

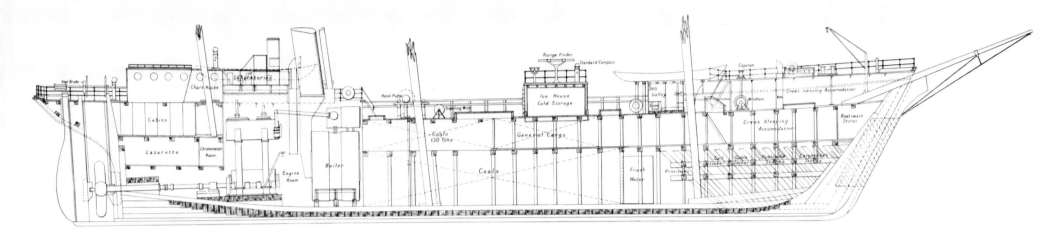

PLAN AT UPPER DECK.

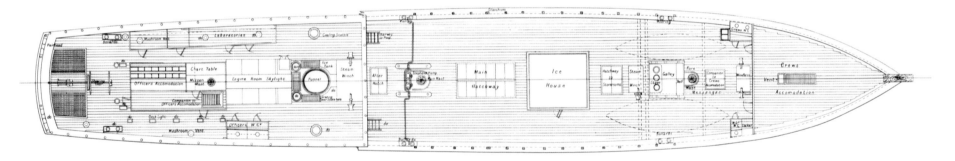

PLAN AT LOWER DECK

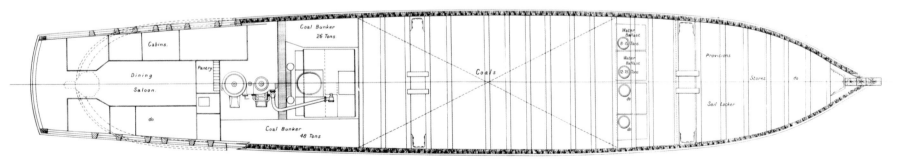

Hunting for seals was nearly as important as hunting for whales for the Dundee Arctic fleet. Seals provided sealskins for leather as well as blubber that would be boiled down into oil. By the middle of the nineteenth century seal hunting often overtook whale hunting in the process of making profit for the Dundee fleet.

In the early period the supply of seals seemed inexhaustible, with shoals of them many miles in extent, but as the nineteenth century wore on, the numbers decreased. Ships had to hunt actively for their prey. However, there were still some respectable catches even in the Greenland Sea, with, for example, *Active* bringing home forty-four tons of seal oil in 1883 and *Esquimaux* catching over 20,000 in 1891. These figures compare favourably with the fifteen seals that were all *Polynia* could manage to bring back from her Greenland voyage in 1872. However, in 1890, Maurice Allard, manager of the Arctic Tannery that made sealskins into leather goods, lived in a splendid house in West Ferry, so the business must have been a success.

This evocative lantern slide reveals two whaling ships searching for seals in an icy sea. The ship nearest has her stern to the camera and is on the right side of the photograph; her sails are furled and she is casting a reflection in the water. The further-away ship also has her sails furled and is viewed from the port quarter. The dangerous conditions in which they worked can clearly be seen.

Overall, at the close of the nineteenth century, Dundee's whaling and sealing ships were arguably the best Arctic vessels of the period. They were purpose-built to work in one of the world's harshest environments and to keep their crews safe. The fact that explorers from other nations sought out Dundee-built vessels for their expeditions speaks volumes about the skill of the shipbuilders of Dundee at that time. It is a legacy of which the city should be proud.

Dis. I.

CERTIFICATE OF DISCHARGE

FOR SEAMEN DISCHARGED BEFORE THE SUPERINTENDENT OF A MERCANTILE MARINE OFFICE IN THE UNITED KINGDOM, A BRITISH CONSUL, OR A SHIPPING OFFICER IN BRITISH POSSESSION ABROAD.

ISSUED BY
THE BOARD OF TRADE
1890.

No. **11**

Name of Ship.	Offic¹. Number.	Port of Registry.	Reg. Tonnage.
Balaena	99205	Dundee	247

Horse Power of Engines (if any).	Description of Voyage or Employment.
66	Antarctic

Name of Seaman.	Age.	Place of Birth.	No. of R. N. R. Commission or Certif.	Capacity. If Mate or Engineer. No. of Cert. (if any)
Isaac McCallum	21	Aberdeen		Sailmaker

Date of Engagement.	Place of Engagement.	Date of Discharge.	Place of Discharge.
6/9/92	Dundee	30/5/93	Dundee

I certify that the above particulars are correct and that the above named Seaman was discharged accordingly,* and that the character described hereon is a true copy of the Report concerning the said Seaman.

Dated this 31 day of May 1893

_____ MASTER.

AUTHENTICATED BY

_____
Signature of Superintendent, Consul, or Shipping Officer

OFFICE
SEAL
OR
OFFICIAL
STAMP.

* If the Seaman does not require a Certificate of his character, obliterate the following Words in lines two and three, and score through the Discs.

CHARACTER
FOR CONDUCT.

CHARACTER
FOR ABILITY.

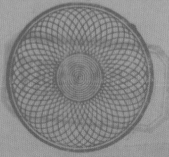

Signature } of Seaman } Isaac McCallum

NOTE.—Any Person who forges or fraudulently alters any Certificate or Report, or who makes use of any Certificate, or Report, which is forged or altered or does not belong to him, shall for each such offence be deemed guilty of a misdemeanor and may be fined or imprisoned.

N.B.—Should this Certificate come into the possession of any person to whom it does not belong it should be handed to the Superintendent of the nearest Mercantile Marine Office, or be transmitted to the Registrar-General of Seamen, Custom House, London, E.C.

WHALING MEN AT WORK AND PLAY

Whaling men were amongst the most adaptable of seamen in the nineteenth century, able to work aloft and on the deck, to row the whaling boats and to process whales and seals. Many men joined as 'Greenmen', or first voyagers, and gradually worked their way up through the ranks to an able seaman, a harpooner or even the master of a ship. When not working hard, whaling men amused themselves with music, cards, dancing and, according to Surgeon Wanless of *Thomas* in 1834, a curious game that involved 'throwing their knives upon the deck into a square divided forty-one times'.

Whaling men could be superstitious or religious, depending on the individual. Surgeon Wanless reported that there were 'religious tracts dealt out' and 'the watch diligently read them', while in 1884, the crew of *Nova Zembla* held prayers and in 1903 the crew of *Diana* sang hymns in the 'tween decks. However, the other side was also present. Wanless also mentioned that the presence of a crow on *Thomas* was reckoned a bad omen and spoke of a belief in witchcraft, while some seamen on *Camperdown* in 1861 believed in mermaids and unlucky days.

Working or at play, religious or superstitious, photographs of whaling men on-board ships in the Arctic seem to be relatively rare, possibly because most ports had ceased whaling by the time

LOG of the S.S. "Aurora" in Lancaster Sound...

H.	Courses.	K.	10ths.	Winds.	Lee Way	Deviation.	Remarks on Saturday the 19 day of July 1884

Wm Adam

Gun & hand harpoons

Bone 10 ft 6"

So & So
Gun
(if harpoon draws)

5 am. Whale seen & all hands sent in pursuit
6 am The mate got fast & the fish took the boats down the Sound
11 am Whale killed & alongside
Noon started to flense
7 p.m. fish on board

Boats crew { W. Adam   Farley
            { Ironsides Balzel
            { Montcliff Walker

19 July, the mate 'got fast', or harpooned the animal, at six o'clock and by eleven the whale was alongside the ship and the crew were flensing her. That was a good day's work that would gain the hands a welcome cash bonus. The half-tail indicates that the ship shared the capture of another whale, so presumably a whaleboat from *Aurora* and a whaleboat from another vessel harpooned and killed the whale simultaneously.

Most whaling ships' log books have been lost or destroyed but those that survive give valuable information about the whaling industry, as well as facts about weather and environmental conditions.

In the eighteenth and nineteenth centuries whaling men often had a fearsome reputation for their behaviour on shore. Some of the images held by Dundee Art Galleries and Museums tend to reinforce this belief.

This photograph shows three whaling seamen posing for the camera. All three are wearing white jackets and are on the deck of a whaling ship. The two bearded men in front are sitting down, while the third, a clean-shaven man, is standing, holding on to a line. However, although they may look truculent, the evidence would suggest that despite the odd mutiny and the occasional brawl or visit to a public house for the occasional refreshment, Dundee's whaling men were no worse than any other seamen.

The museum holds images of whaling men with their wives as well as documents that prove they paid a large part of their wages to their wives, which was hardly the action of wild men.

photography became popular (or affordable). Because of that, Dundee Art Galleries and Museums are in a unique position of being able to offer a selection of images that could have an appeal well beyond the bounds of Dundee.

From 1733 until 1824, whaling-ship owners could claim an official government bounty to offset some of the cost of the voyage. However, there were stipulations. The ship had to carry a number of Greenmen so they could gain seagoing experience, the master and owner had to swear an oath that they were sailing to the whaling grounds, and they had to keep a detailed log.

This lantern slide shows one page of the log of the Dundee whaling ship *Aurora* in July 1884, a time when the Dundee whaling fleet was at its height. The image of the whale's tail signifies that the ship caught a whale that day. The text alongside states that the crew sighted a whale at five in the morning of the

Among the specialists that Dundee whaling vessels carried on board was a carpenter who dealt with any damage to the fabric of the vessel, a sail maker to make and repair the sails, an engineer who maintained and worked the engines and a blacksmith. The blacksmith was responsible for any work that involved the metal parts of the ship, as well as checking and sharpening the tools used for capturing and killing whales and seals. In 1880 the blacksmith on the Dundee ship *Intrepid* was paid £3 a month.

This photograph opposite was taken on the deck of an unidentified whaling vessel. It was taken from amidships looking aft and shows the mizzen mast and funnel of the vessel. In the foreground is the blacksmith and some of the tools of his trade. The anvil and bellows can be clearly seen. The smith would use a file to sharpen the iron harpoons and lances, and straighten them on the anvil if they had been warped and bent by a whale. The harpoon was used to secure and hold the whale until it tired itself out towing the six-man whale boat, while the lance was used to deliver the fatal blow that actually killed the animal. When the whale was brought back to the ship, the crew would flense it. The blacksmith would have ensured that the flensing tools were sharp enough to do the job.

The blacksmith is wearing the white jacket and fur hat that was nearly a uniform for the Dundee whaling men. The photograph was taken towards the close of the nineteenth century or the beginning of the twentieth.

To ensure they ran efficiently, Dundee whaling vessels carried a number of specialists. These included sail makers, carpenters and blacksmiths. Although this sepia print appears posed, it does give an idea of the bustle and atmosphere on the deck of a nineteenth-century whaling ship even when there was no whaling in progress.

T. F. Miller took this photograph in 1876, when Dundee was one of the two leading whaling ports in Great Britain. The bearded carpenter is sawing a length of wood, while a younger man sits on a barrel and strokes a dog. The barrel could hold stores such as flour, or perhaps would later be filled with blubber from a whale or a seal. A ship's boy is sitting on deck; he might be thirteen or fourteen years old, which was the accepted age for boys on their first whaling voyage. Presumably the man on the right was the blacksmith. Judging by the dress of the men, the vessel is not yet in the Arctic so could be on the outward voyage.

In the eighteenth and nineteenth centuries, seamen from whaling ships sometimes had an unenviable reputation for boisterous behaviour when they were ashore and sometimes also at sea. There were a number of mutinies on Dundee whaling ships; there was one on *Fairy* in 1842 when the crew thought the master was inexperienced, another by some men of *Intrepid* in Iceland in 1883 and a third by the crew of *Diana* in 1892. There was also a major dispute about wages in early 1892. Whaling men were not afraid to stand up for their rights.

Given the international nature of maritime life, a surprising number of Dundee whaling seamen were local. In a random sample of 200 seamen on Dundee ships in the nineteenth century, ninety-two were from Dundee and Broughty Ferry, twenty-one from Peterhead, twenty-three from Shetland and nineteen from Fife, with the remainder from various places.

Captain Andrew Shewan, who commanded clipper ships in the days of the tea races, hired some ex-whaling men and in his book *The Great Days of Sail* wrote about their 'truculence of demeanour' and thought they were 'by no means easy to manage'. This lantern slide depicts a group of five men on the deck of a Dundee whaling ship around the end of the nineteenth century. The light jackets were normal wear for many Dundee whaling men, while the grim expressions suggest men whom it was best not to provoke.

From the 1860s many Dundee whaling ships made two voyages a year. The first usually began in February and visited the Greenland Sea around the islands of Spitsbergen or Nova Zembla. The second was from Dundee to St John's in Newfoundland. The first recorded Dundee whaling voyage to St John's was in 1862, with *Camperdown* and *Polynia*. Although that attempt was a disaster, it encouraged St John's entrepreneurs to purchase Dundee-built sealing ships. In 1876 Captain Adams brought *Arctic* over and began a period of direct Dundee participation in Newfoundland sealing. Adams thought the Newfoundlanders 'very smart men' and thereafter Dundee vessels would recruit a large number of these *sweilers* – local seal hunters – from St John's and would hunt whales in the Davis Strait and seals along the coasts of Newfoundland and Labrador. Another Dundee whaling master, James Fairweather,

thought the Newfoundlanders 'perfectly wonderful in the way they jumped from pan to pan'. In March 1877 the Newfoundland *Morning Chronicle* commented: 'We do not exclude our Dundee friends . . . the fact that *Arctic* and *Aurora* are manned by nearly 500 of our men calls for our very best wishes respecting them.'

Captain William Gray took this lantern slide that shows the harbour of St John's when it was busy with shipping. Such a sight would be familiar to Dundee seamen. The Dundee Seal and Whale Fishing Company purchased land in St John's and erected a blubber-boiling works as well as storage facilities. The two towns had a very close working relationship until 1900.

As mentioned above, in the early nineteenth century British whaling vessels often made a rendezvous at Disko Island off the west coast of Greenland. From there they sailed north past

the strange rock formation known as the Devil's Thumb before heading across Melville Bay to the whale fishing grounds of the West Water.

In 1830, the voyage across Melville Bay turned into a disaster. Fifty ships gathered at the Devil's Thumb and waited for the ice to retreat. When a narrow crack appeared, the ships threaded their way westward. However, the ice closed on the fleet. Nineteen British ships were wrecked and the crews were stranded on the ice. Rather than despair, the whaling men broke into the spirit stores of the sinking ships and spent days in a drunken spree. This affair, alluded to earlier, was known as the Baffin Fair. Not all the whaling men approved; the master of *St Andrew* of Aberdeen said, 'Many of the shipwrecked crews were insubordinate.'

This watercolour by John Gowland is on display in Dundee Art Galleries and Museums. It possibly shows the Baffin Fair. It depicts a whaling fleet trapped in ice with some ships sinking and men camping on the ice. Gowland was a seaman as well as an artist, so he would probably have heard of the incident at first hand.

Sealing was an important side of the whaling industry. One hunting ground for the sealers was in the Greenland Sea, around the islands of Jan Mayen Land and Spitsbergen, once known as East Greenland. While a sail-powered vessel could spend a month on the passage to the sealing grounds, the later steam ships could cut that time in half. By the late 1870s it was normal for Dundee vessels to seal in the Greenland Sea first, return to Dundee and then sail across the Atlantic to St John's in Newfoundland. They would recruit a crew of local *sweilers* to hunt seals on the banks of Newfoundland and Labrador.

As late as the 1840s sealers thought the supplies of seals were unlimited, as they found shoals that stretched as far as the lookout in the crow's nest could see in either direction. By the 1870s the numbers had dwindled, so the Dundee sealers backed the government-sponsored close season. Their efforts concentrated on Labrador and Newfoundland.

Seal hunters were most active from March until June. They operated on the pack ice where seals congregated, shot or clubbed the seals and dragged the skins into depots known as 'pans'. Each ship marked their pan with a flag. The numbers of seals killed was frightening; for example, in 1878 alone *Arctic II* captured 33,000 seals.

This lantern slide shows sealers establishing a seal pan in the ice. Many men carry a long staff to check how secure the ice is and to aid them walking.

Seal hunting had been important to the whaling industry from at least the eighteenth century. For example, in 1787 *Dundee* of Dundee brought home 1,500 seals and *Tay* of Dundee 1,400. Seals were hunted for their skins as well as for the blubber that was boiled down into oil. Sealers waited at the edge of the ice until the seal pups were weaned and therefore mature enough to warrant killing.

The mature seals were usually shot and the younger seals clubbed to death. The seal clubs were ferocious, two-handed weapons that often had a long spike at the back. The seals then were usually skinned on the spot and the skins stored in a 'pan'. This was nothing more than a pile of sealskin with the ship's flag

waving above to mark which ship owned the seals. As soon as the hunters had collected sufficient sealskins, or when there were no more seals to be found, they dragged the skins back to the ship with a 'lowery tow', which was a rope about three metres long and about three centimetres in diameter. It was not unknown for the men to haul the bundles for miles, and with a mature skin weighing up to 50kg, sealing was hard work. When they reached the ship the skins were stripped of their blubber, which was a skilled job. Sealskins sold at around 12.5p each and had a variety of uses.

In the times they were not actively hunting, whaling men were often busy about the ship. Even before the whaling grounds were reached the seamen had to keep the whaleboats seaworthy and ensure that the harpoons, lances and lines were ready in case the lookout spotted a whale. On the voyages to and from the ice, the seamen had to perform the ordinary shipboard duties, but in addition to hunting they had to flense the whales and the seals and pack the blubber away.

This lantern slide by F. Livingstone-Learmonth shows a seaman sitting on deck and splicing a foreganger line onto a gun harpoon.

The foreganger line – the line that 'went before' – attached the harpoon to the actual whale line. The split shaft of the harpoon was only used for a gun harpoon, while hand-held weapons had a single shaft. The seaman is wearing the white jacket that was common among Dundee whaling men and he is working with a 'fid', a long spike rather like a large knitting needle. The ropes beside him are the whale lines. They were coiled very carefully in the whaleboats so they would not kink when the harpooned whale swam away. It was the task of a line manager to ensure the lines on the whaleboat were stored and used correctly.

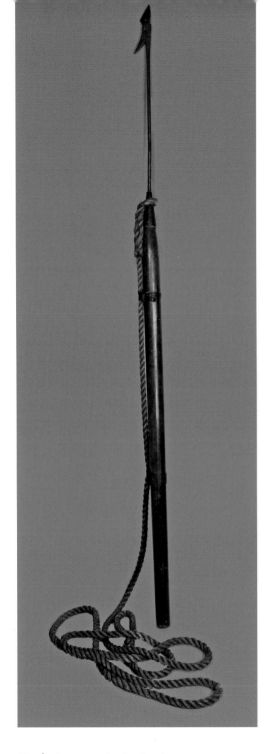

Possibly the tool most frequently associated with whaling men is the harpoon. This example is held in Dundee Art Galleries and Museums. It is a hand harpoon with a small, single-fluked head. The head has a swivelling barb, so it could enter the animal smoothly but the barb would extend to prevent it falling out. Unusually after such a passage of time, this harpoon still has the foreganger attached. As previously mentioned, the foreganger is the length of rope that connects the harpoon to the line that stretches back to the whaleboat.

The harpooner would use both hands to thrust the harpoon deep inside the whale. His job was one of the most important in the ship but his exploits were usually only mentioned very briefly in logs or journals. For example, Captain Thomas Davidson's *A Journal of a Voyage from Dundee Towards Davis Strait On Board the Dorothy* records that on 21 September 1834 'William Latto got fast to a whale.' In this case 'fast' meant that William Latto the harpooner was successful in harpooning the whale. Dundee Museum has notes of a William Latto, who rose through the ranks to become a harpooner on *Dorothy*, so presumably that was the same man. William Latto was one of the few survivors when *Thomas* was trapped in the ice in season 1836–37.

The harpoon was not used to kill the whale; it merely attached the whale to the whaleboat. The whale tired itself out towing a number of whaleboats and eventually halted, floating on the surface. When it did so the whaling men would close. They approached from behind the whale and to the side. When they were close enough, the harpooners would kill the whale with sharp lances.

The crux of every whaling voyage was the killing of the whale. If the harpooner was sufficiently skilled he would be able to plunge the harpoon deep inside the whale. After that his primary job was done. The harpooner was one of the highest-paid men on board the ship. In 1832 Robert Ogilvie and Robert Adamson, harpooners on the Dundee vessel *Dorothy*, earned £1 a month plus a bonus that depended on the amount of whale oil and baleen the ship brought home. That same year an ordinary seaman earned 15 shillings a month, with lesser amounts for his bonus. It was worthwhile learning the skills of a harpooner.

The entire crew would celebrate if a harpooner was successful, but killing the whale could be difficult. Once the harpoon was embedded in the whale, the oarsmen rapidly backed water, for the animal would lash its tail; even a glancing blow from the flukes could sink a whaleboat. It was more likely for the whale to dive or 'sound', which meant it would submerge and swim away at some speed. Even if the harpooner was successful, there was no guarantee that the whale would be caught, for the animal would twist and turn to escape.

The harpoon in this photograph is held by Dundee Art Galleries and Museums. The shank has been twisted by a whale during its struggle to free itself. The double shank shows that it was fired from a gun rather than launched by hand. Often made in Dundee, harpoons were always of the best-quality iron so they would bend rather than break.

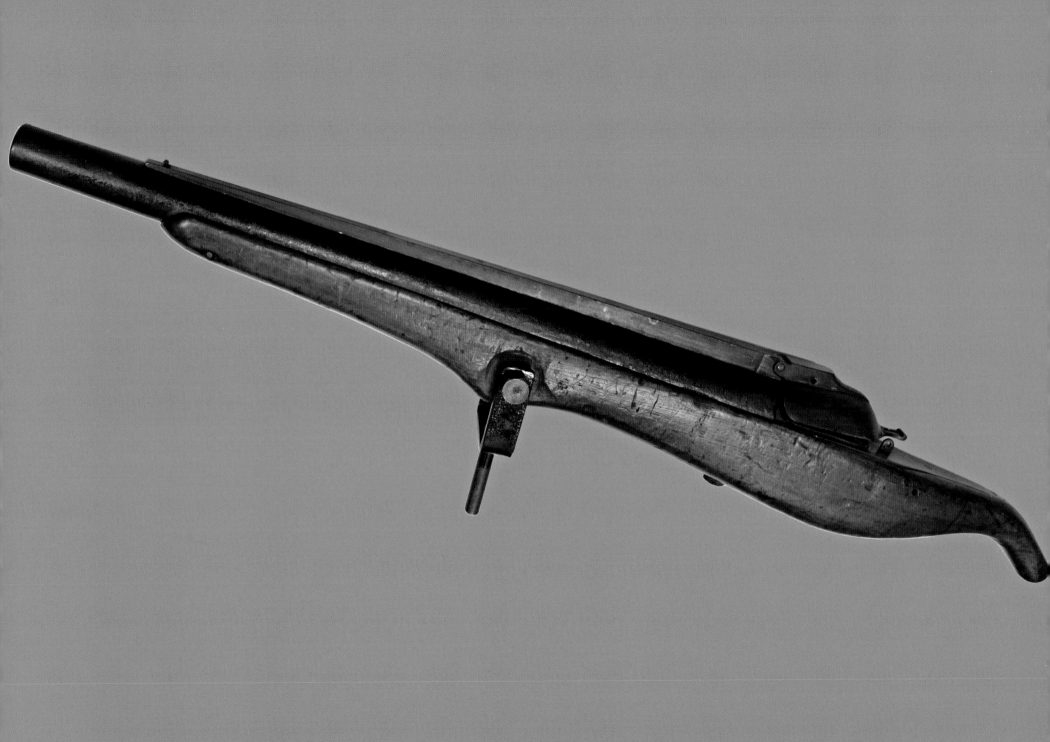

For much of the life of the whaling industry, harpooners stood in the bows of the boat and hurled the harpoon at the whale. However, the whaling men searched for a more efficient method of catching whales. There had been attempts to create a harpoon gun from at least 1731, but as contemporary technology only extended to a flintlock, the gun was not efficient in nautical conditions. The flintlock mechanism worked by a flint striking a piece of metal and the resulting spark igniting gunpowder. The explosion of the powder propelled the harpoon forward. In 1751 the Leith ship *Tryal* carried a device for throwing harpoons, the details of which have been lost.

In 1772 the Society of Arts Manufacturers and Commerce offered a twenty-guinea reward for improvements to the whaling gun, and in 1790 it was realised that a cover over the flintlock mechanism would help keep out the worst of the wet. In 1837 William Greener of Riflehill Works in Birmingham had invented a workable percussion harpoon gun known as the Greener Gun. A weapon such as this would be mounted in the bows of a whaleboat, with a line attached from a metal ring on the actual harpoon to the boat. These guns had a range of up to eighty-four yards and could fire across ice floes, so it increased the distance from which a whale could be caught. It used large-grain gunpowder for the percussion cap, so the burn was slow and the harpoon's flight steady.

The version pictured here has a wooden stock and steel barrel, with brass sights and firing mechanism. The sight has 'Arctic N4 Dundee 1875' on it so may have been used on *Arctic II*, which was launched in Dundee in 1875.

floated on the surface and the men readied it for the tow back to the ship. They would fasten the fins beneath the whale so it was streamlined, then thread a cable through the flukes to the boat. With the whale secured, the men would begin the pull back to the whaling ship. Sometimes the men would sing as they rowed, with 'Highland Laddie' apparently a favourite song. If there had been more than one whaleboat involved in the hunt, the labour was correspondingly easier.

This lantern slide shows a group of men in two whaleboats beside a whale's tail. The men are trying to manipulate the tail, presumably getting it prepared for the tow back to the ship.

Once the whale was towed back to the ship it was processed. That meant the jaw bone was removed and taken on board, so the baleen or 'whalebone' could be removed, and the blubber was stripped from the body. This latter process was hard work. It was preferable to flense during periods of good weather, for heavy seas could sweep away a captured whale.

With the whale alongside, the *spectioneer* – head harpooner – supervised as men fitted spurs on their boots so they would not slip. They then stood on the whale and stripped the blubber with long flensing knives. They first took a strip of blubber from around the neck and then used a windlass to turn the whale slowly around as they sliced off the blubber. A block and tackle would probably be used to hoist the blubber on board.

This photograph by Walter Livingstone-Learmonth shows something of the flensing operation. The whaleboat in the foreground has brought a whale to the Dundee ship *Eclipse*. The harpoon gun in the bows of the boat can be seen quite clearly. The whale is between the boat and the hull of *Eclipse*. This photograph was taken in 1888 when *Eclipse* sailed from Peterhead.

Although whaling ships have the fame, they were only transports and store vessels. Whaling men hunted from small boats known as whaleboats. These vessels were open to the elements and powered by sail and oar. Each was about twenty-six feet in length and carried a crew of six. There were three officers: a harpooner who threw the harpoon, a boatsteerer who steered to the whale and a line manager who looked after the line that connected the harpooned whale to the boat. The other members of the crew were oarsmen.

A harpooned whale could drag the boat for miles; the Whitby whaling master William Scoresby mentioned a hunt that lasted forty hours. However, when a whale was eventually killed it

Terra Nova was one of the most successful of all Dundee whaling vessels. When this lantern slide was taken in 1894, she was commanded by Harry McKay. That year *Terra Nova* operated from St John's Newfoundland and hunted in the Davis Strait. She captured over 7,000 seals, three black whales and five white whales. Captain William Gray is credited with this picture that shows one of the black whales being flensed. Two of the whaleboats can be seen on the outside of the whale, with the whaling gun clearly visible in the bows. There are two similar guns held in the whaling collection in Dundee Museum. The whaling men are just about to start work stripping the blubber. This was the climax of the whaler's work, but by the 1890s whales were not easy to catch. In the earlier decades of the century Dundee vessels had returned with up to thirty-seven whales, but overhunting had seen a terrible decline in whale numbers.

The Dundee Arctic whaling industry only had another twenty years of life left and *Terra Nova* was the last Dundee-built ship to be used by the Dundee whalers.

The crew of the whaleboat was fixed at the start of the voyage so each man knew exactly where to go when a whale was sighted. There were two types of harpooners, 'fast' and 'loose', with 'fast' harpooners being experienced men who were assigned a boat and 'loose' harpooners being a mobile reserve, ready to step in if needed.

As well as a harpooner there was a boatsteerer and a line manager. These three men were paid higher rates than the other crewmen, with a boatsteerer earning £3 a month in 1874 compared to an ordinary seaman's £2 a month. Their bonuses for the amount of whale oil and baleen the ship brought home were also higher.

This picture shows two whaleboats forming a 'Vee' with the hull of the whaling ship *Eclipse*. There are blocks attached to the whale that floats within the Vee, presumably to turn it for the flensing process. The man standing on the whale will be bearing spurs on his boots so that he does not slip, while the whale gun in the nearest of the two whaleboats can be seen quite clearly.

At times the deck of an Arctic whaling ship could be very busy. This photograph shows some of the crew cutting whale blubber into cubes to be stored down below. This process was known as 'making off'. The bustle shows just how crowded the deck of a nineteenth-century whaling ship could be when up to fifty men were working on board. It is a reminder that a whaling ship was also a floating factory for processing whales, seals and other Arctic animals for commercial gain.

This photograph was taken by a Broughty Ferry photographer named Francis Gillies. In 1900 he signed on the Dundee whaling ship *Diana* as a crewman, claiming the voyage was for the good of his health. On the voyage he became involved in the barter of a Martini Henry rifle with the Inuit, which was contrary to the articles he signed. The case came to court. Gillies took a number of photographs on the voyage, some of which are held by Dundee Art Galleries and Museums.

Diana was a Norwegian-built vessel that was in the Dundee fleet from 1892 until 1915. In 1892 she was part of the Dundee Antarctic Expedition. On the 1900 voyage, with Robert Davidson as master, she killed six whales, fifty-four walruses and twenty-four bears.

Dismantling and stowing away the pieces of an animal as large as a whale was a messy and complex procedure that took many man hours. Once the blubber was flensed from the whale it was brought on board the ship to be processed. In common with other merchant seamen, whaling men were highly skilled in manoeuvring heavy objects by using the spars of the ship with an arrangement of block and tackle to increase the mechanical power.

Captain William Gray is reputed to have taken this photograph. It shows the cant piece – a large slice of whale blubber about ten metres long – at the masthead of a whaling ship. It is being lowered to the deck where it will be 'made off'. The picture (left) reveals just how large the cant was when compared to the men who are working with it.

Once a whale had been flensed, the blubber was hoisted on board the whaling ship by means of block and tackle. The crew would then chop it into rough cubes and pack it away. In the earlier whaling ships the blubber was held in casks which were stowed in the hold. By around 1870 most Dundee vessels were purpose-built with large iron tanks specially constructed for holding blubber.

Taken in 1894, this photograph (right) shows crewmen of the Dundee ship *Active* chopping blubber. They are working at low tables and some are wearing the fur hats that were common in whaling vessels during that period. The flensing and subsequent disposal of the blubber was a filthy job but the men would not mind, as the longer they worked the more money they made. They were paid a fixed wage plus a bonus that could easily double the money they brought home. The blubber would be taken back to Dundee to be boiled into oil, which was used to soften jute in Dundee's many mills. That year oil was selling at around £20 a ton.

Active was a very successful vessel, being in the Dundee whaling fleet from 1874 until whaling from Dundee ceased. She was sunk during the First World War.

This photograph shows the upper jaw of a whale being lowered onto the deck of a Dundee whaling ship. From the size of the bone, the whale was quite a catch. Such animals became a scarcity in the later years of the industry, as the whaling vessels had to penetrate deeper into the ice to make their voyages profitable. The curve of the jawbone can be seen at the top of the picture, while the whalebone, or baleen, hangs down in long strips. These lengths of baleen are around two centimetres apart and are made of keratin, a material that also forms nails, hair and the horns of cattle. There are a number of crewmen in the picture, facing the camera.

Baleen was one of the two products that made whale hunting profitable. The other product was the blubber that was boiled into oil. Baleen was used to make a large number of items, from chair backs to sprigs and nets, but it was perhaps best known for its use in the women's fashion industry. Stays and stiffeners in corsets, bonnets and bodices, hoops for crinolines and spokes for umbrellas: baleen was used for them all. The price of baleen fluctuated throughout the whaling period, with a high of £2,900 a ton in 1903 compared to £720 a ton in 1881. In 1882 alone thirty tons were brought into Dundee, earning over £35,000 for the industry.

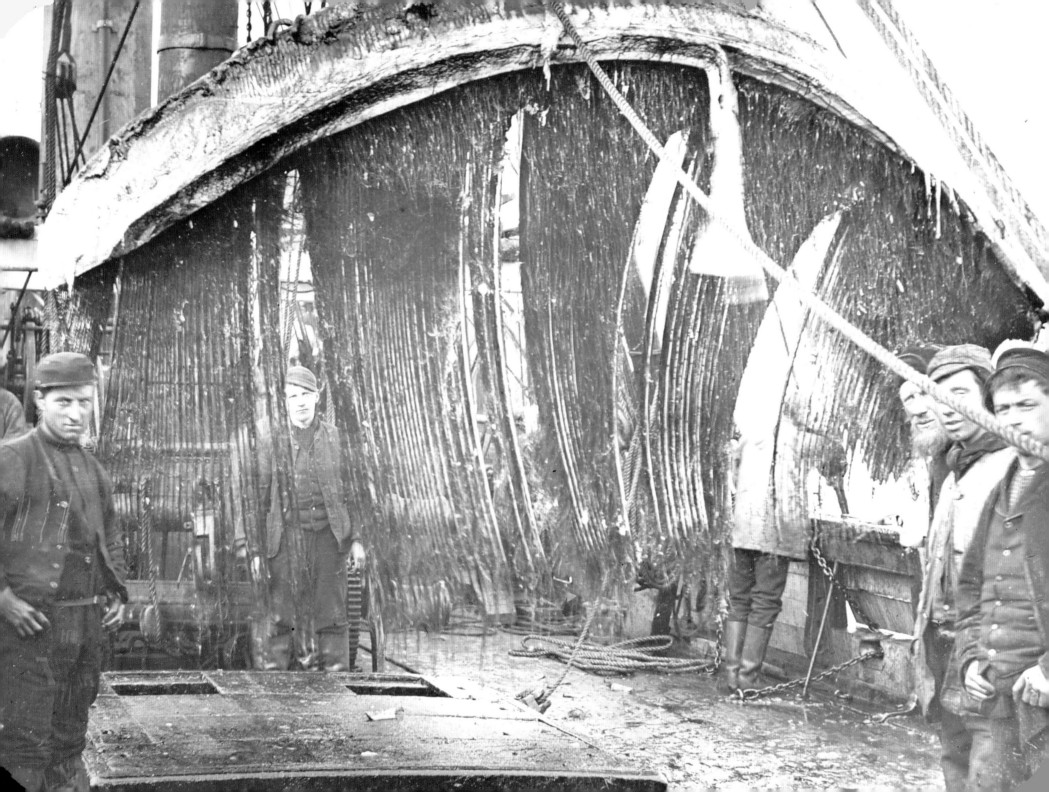

Hunting was a passion for many men in the nineteenth century. Even as big-game hunters scoured the world for trophies and aristocrats slaughtered deer in the Scottish Highlands, whaling ships sailed to the Arctic in search of profitable prey. As well as whales and seals, whaling ships also hunted narwhals, belugas, polar bears and walruses. While the indigenous peoples of the Arctic hunted walruses to obtain meat for their dogs, Europeans sought the walruses for their ivory tusks. However, at one time bicycle owners preferred walrus skins to any other for keeping their machines shiny and clean. Between 1867 and 1911 Dundee vessels killed over 10,000 walruses. In 1867 *Arctic* brought home a live walrus that was sold to Regent's Park Zoo in London for an estimated £200.

This picture shows a member of the crew of a whaling ship cutting tusks from the skull of a walrus. He is wearing the white jacket and fur cap that could nearly be termed a uniform for whaling men. Cutting out walrus tusks was a skilled job, as one slip of the axe could damage the ivory and therefore reduce its value.

Whaling ships were expected to make a profit for their owners. Their prime concern was catching whales for the blubber that was boiled into oil, and for baleen that had many different uses. Prices for baleen, also known as whalebone, fluctuated throughout the whaling period. For example, in 1824 it sold at £125 a ton, £150 a ton in 1833, £315 a ton in 1856 and £2,200 a ton in 1884. After that it dipped considerably, only to rise again in 1901 when the United States whaling industry failed.

The lantern slide (left) shows two members of a whaling crew splitting baleen. That means they were cutting it into manageable lengths. The tool they are using is very similar to one that is held in Dundee Art Galleries and Museums. Walter Livingstone-Learmonth took this photograph on *Eclipse* in 1888, when she sailed from Peterhead.

Whaling men were unlike any other type of seamen. As well as the normal nautical skills of knotwork and setting and furling sails in a screaming Atlantic gale, they were expert in small boat work in fog and ice. Augmenting those skills was their expertise in hunting whales and seals and their interpersonal skills with the Inuit. They often worked on land as well as at sea, catching salmon or trapping the Arctic animals, picking up stores from local depots and even working dog sleds. The Dundee whaling men were jacks of all trades and masters of many.

The lantern slide to the right shows a seaman from a Dundee whaling ship setting traps in the ice. Despite the obvious cold he seems to be wearing ordinary nautical clothing. They bred them tough in Dundee in those days. Whaling was a multi-skilled job in the late nineteenth century and the Dundee seaman was arguably the most skilled Arctic whaling man in the world.

Whaling ships hunted for many types of species in the Arctic. The prime target was the bowhead whale or Greenland right whale, the *Balaena mysticetus*, which they termed a black whale. However, they also hunted belugas and narwhals, both of which the whaling men termed as white whales. The name narwhal is from the Norse 'nar' or corpse whale and refers to its white colour; they are usually found north of 65° latitude. Dundee whaling men often referred to them as 'unicorns' or 'unis'. In 1908 alone, Dundee whaling ships caught 540 white whales.

This image shows a narwhal lying on the deck of a whaling ship. Although it is one of the medium-sized types of whale, it dwarfs the crewmen who are standing next to it. The block and tackle to the left of the narwhal may have helped bring the animal on deck, while the open hatch cover may indicate that after the narwhal was processed, the blubber would be stowed below.

Narwhals were also prized for their long horns, which are in reality an extremely extended tooth. Male tusks are longer and without the spiral effect of female tusks. These were often carved into walking sticks. Dundee Art Galleries and Museums hold a number of these beautiful objects in their whaling collection.

By the late nineteenth century, Arctic whaling was falling on hard times. Catches were down, whales and seals were increasingly elusive and whaling companies were looking for alternative means of scratching a profit.

The Arctic provided a number of different wildlife products, including wild salmon. This photograph shows a group of seamen gutting salmon on the deck of a whaling ship. In the foreground there are two men, each carrying two salmon. Behind them is a row of men working at a table, with boxes of fish on the deck in front of them. There seems to be no record existing of any impact Arctic salmon made in Dundee, so it is possible the fish were not carried all the way to Scotland but might have been sold at St John's Newfoundland. It is something on which further research may be done.

Seamen were often independent minded and if conditions on board a ship were not to their liking, they would leave at the next port or simply desert. Obviously this created problems for the masters of ships, so a system gradually evolved whereby seamen were issued with certificates that proved they had been officially discharged. These discharge certificates also acted as a form of identification and statement of character.

The first known discharge certificates were issued in the eighteenth century and the documents became compulsory in 1835, while the 1854 Merchant Shipping Act made the system more complex and formal. Men who had served in foreign-going vessels, such as the Dundee whaling ships, who were discharged in the UK used 'E-1' forms. This certificate of discharge is held in Dundee Art Galleries and Museums. It was issued to Mr Isaac McCallum on 31 May 1893 and provides a great deal of information. It states that Mr McCallum was aged twenty-one and had been born in Aberdeen. It also said he had been engaged as a sail maker in the Dundee-registered, 247-ton *Balaena* between 6 September 1892 and 30 May 1893, on a voyage to the Antarctic. The ship's master, Alexander Fairweather, signed at the bottom of the certificate, giving Mr McCallum a character of 'very good' for both conduct and ability.

Dis. I.

CERTIFICATE OF DISCHARGE

FOR SEAMEN DISCHARGED BEFORE THE SUPERINTENDENT OF A MERCANTILE
MARINE OFFICE IN THE UNITED KINGDOM, A BRITISH CONSUL, OR A SHIPPING
OFFICER IN BRITISH POSSESSION ABROAD.

ISSUED BY
THE BOARD OF TRADE
1890.

No. **11**

Name of Ship.	Offic¹. Number.	Port of Registry.	Reg. Tonnage.
Balaena	99205	Dundee	247

Horse Power of Engines (if any).	Description of Voyage or Employment.
66	Antarctic

Name of Seaman.	Age.	Place of Birth.	No. of R. N. R. Commission or Certif.	Capacity. If Mate or Engineer. No. of Cert. (if any).
Isaac McCallum	21	Aberdeen		Sailmaker

Date of Engagement.	Place of Engagement.	Date of Discharge.	Place of Discharge.
6/9/92	Dundee	30/5/93	Dundee

I certify that the above particulars are correct and that the above named
Seaman was discharged accordingly,* and that the character described hereon
is a true copy of the Report concerning the said Seaman.

Dated this 31 day of May 1893

~~Alex Fairweather~~ MASTER.

AUTHENTICATED BY

Signature of Superintendent, Consul, or Shipping Officer

OFFICE
SEAL
OR
OFFICIAL
STAMP.

* If the Seaman does not require a Certificate of his character, obliterate the following Words in lines two and three, and score through the Discs.

**CHARACTER
FOR CONDUCT.**

**CHARACTER
FOR ABILITY.**

Signature of Seaman } Isaac McCallum

Kinnes also operated a whaling and trading station in the Arctic. The slide (left) may illustrate that station, as the Kinnes House flag of a single star is flying from the roof. This flag was also worn by ships of the Kinnes fleet. The station would be home to a representative of the Tay Whale Fishing Company throughout the year. Furs and whale oil or blubber would be stored here, together with any other Arctic produce. A ship would periodically call from Dundee to take away the produce and replenish the goods the post used to barter with the local Inuit.

In the year 1900 the Broughty Ferry photographer Francis Gillies signed on the whaling ship *Diana* as a member of the crew. A number of the photographs he took have been carefully preserved in Dundee Art Galleries and Museums.

The photograph to the right shows two of *Diana's* supply boats ashore in the Arctic. As only the second boat is occupied, presumably the crewmen are at one of the Arctic settlements collecting supplies for the ship. By the late nineteenth century it was unusual for most seamen to also be skilled in small boat work, but whaling seamen were expected to be able to turn their hands to a variety of tasks. They were among the most skilled seamen anywhere and worked in often terrible conditions, but a successful whaling voyage could be very remunerative. The seaman in the second boat appears casually confident in his position. He is wearing clothes that seem inadequate for the icy conditions, which suggests an element of the toughness that Dundee whaling men were famed for, and he is smoking either a cigarette or a pipe. Cigarettes had become more popular since the Crimean War (1854–1856) and in 1900 the newspapers lauded them as helping the defenders of Mafeking. How trends change!

The company of Robert Kinnes and Sons was formed in 1883 as a trading name for the Tay Whale Fishing Company. From that date the Kinnes family dominated Dundee and therefore British Arctic whaling. It was the Tay Whale Fishing Company that organised the Dundee Antarctic Whaling Expedition in 1892. This was a four-ship voyage that was accomplished with the minimum of fuss and casualties compared with many government-sponsored expeditions of the same era. On that expedition, Cape Kinnes on Joinville Island off north-east Antarctica was named by the Dundee whaling men.

Mariners have always been renowned for bringing souvenirs home from their travels. Exotic animals and birds have been a favourite for centuries, and the Dundee whaling men were no exception. As whales and seals were worth more dead than alive, these animals did not make it back to Scotland. It would have been difficult to transport a live whale but no doubt the ingenuity of the Dundee seamen would have managed somehow. However, it was common for Dundee whaling masters to present the museum with specimens from the Arctic. In 1879, for instance, Captain McLennan of *Narwhal* presented a stuffed polar bear. Two years later, Captain Adams of *Arctic* went one better and brought home a live polar bear. In 1891 *Active* brought home a young polar bear, which was later sent to Hamburg, and the artist Burn Murdoch also brought home a polar bear cub, which he named Starboard and handed to the Zoological Society of Scotland.

It would be good to think that this young polar bear, photographed as it peers over the rim of an oil cask, was looked after kindly. With so many bears being transported, however, it is unlikely that this little bear's ultimate fate will ever be known.

By the beginning of the twentieth century, explorers were opening up the Arctic and frequently exploiting what their experiences had been. One of these was Sandon Perkins, a fellow of the Royal Geographical Society, whom was mentioned briefly before. He travelled the world, from the Carnegie Hall in New York to Otago in New Zealand, giving illustrated talks on his travels. One of his talks, 'Midst Arctic Snows', was heard by an estimated half a million people across four continents. In 1916 the *Daily News* of London commented that Perkins 'is a delightful lecturer and those, old and young, who will hear what he has to say will never forget the story'.

However, Perkins sometimes over-reached himself. When he was lecturing to the Liverpool Geographical Society in the summer of 1909 he stated that the North Pole would be reached by aeroplane and said he hoped to lead his own aerial exploration the next year.

This lantern slide shows Perkins on board the Dundee whaling ship *Morning*. He is suitably dressed for an Arctic expedition, although one can only guess what the Dundee seamen thought of him. Presumably the photograph was taken in 1906 when Perkins accompanied *Morning* on her voyage to the Davis Strait.

Scotland had long been a sporting nation. Mary, Queen of Scots played golf and billiards, while horse and foot racing had been a Scottish pastime for centuries; shinty was as old as time, and in the early nineteenth-century cricket was common and nearly every town had at least one curling pond. But by the 1870s a new passion had arrived: football.

In an article written for *The Scots Magazine*, Captain James Fairweather mentioned that in 1875 the Dundee whaling men were all 'fitba mad'. Each of the ships had their own football teams that competed with each other either on land or on the ice. Fairweather mentioned one occasion when ships' teams played on the ice in the Davis Strait. Possibly it was the scent of the sealskin football that attracted a polar bear, but both teams had to run to the nearest vessel and clamber up a single swinging ladder before the bear caught up with them.

This illustration is of the team of the Dundee whaling ship *Active* posing on the ice. Possibly the descendants of these men played at Dens Park or Tannadice; if so, it is good to think they learned their skills in such an interesting environment. The photograph was taken off Spitsbergen in 1894 and the poles carried by two of the men may have been to probe for holes in the ice, or could be the goalposts.

Scrimshaw is an art form whereby designs are carved on whalebone or ivory. It is also a nautical word meaning 'to waste time', which suggests that the early whaling seamen who carved such designs may not always have been the most popular men on board. Many genuine examples of scrimshaw were created by whaling men on long voyages, with American and British South Seas whalers carving on sperm teeth and Arctic whaling men preferring baleen, although other materials were also used.

However, scrimshaw was practised by the native Inuit of the Arctic long before the arrival of whaling ships from Europe or North America. Some of the early Inuit work may have had religious significance. When the whaling men were in the Arctic they would often barter with the Inuit, and presumably this piece found its way to Dundee by those means.

This particular piece is Inuit work on walrus ivory. It shows an Inuit in a kayak harpooning a seal lying on an ice floe. It is unfortunate that the piece is not complete, for it is a fine example of the art form. There is a large market for scrimshaw today but many pieces are modern and have no connection to either whaling or the Inuit.

In 1883 one brave whale had the audacity to enter the Firth of Tay at a time when Dundee was the most significant whale-hunting port in the United Kingdom. Although the whaling fleet was laid up for the winter, a number of men immediately tried to capture the forty-one-foot-long whale. With a number of harpoons stuck in it, the whale beat a hasty retreat out of the Firth, towing two six-oared boats, a steam ferry and a steam tug in its mad dash to freedom. The whale dragged them north to Montrose, south to the Firth of Forth and then north again. By that time the wind had risen and the lines attaching the whale to the boats snapped and it escaped. Unfortunately the damage had been done and the whale died. Fishermen found it floating off Inverbervie and they towed it to Stonehaven. A Dundee oil merchant named John Woods, better known as 'Greasy Johnny', paid £226 for the carcass. A tug towed the whale back to Dundee, where it took twenty horses, a very strong cart and twenty-six hours of hard labour to transport it to Johnny's oil yard. This photograph by Charles Johnson of Dundee's Nethergate shows a crane lifting the whale ashore.

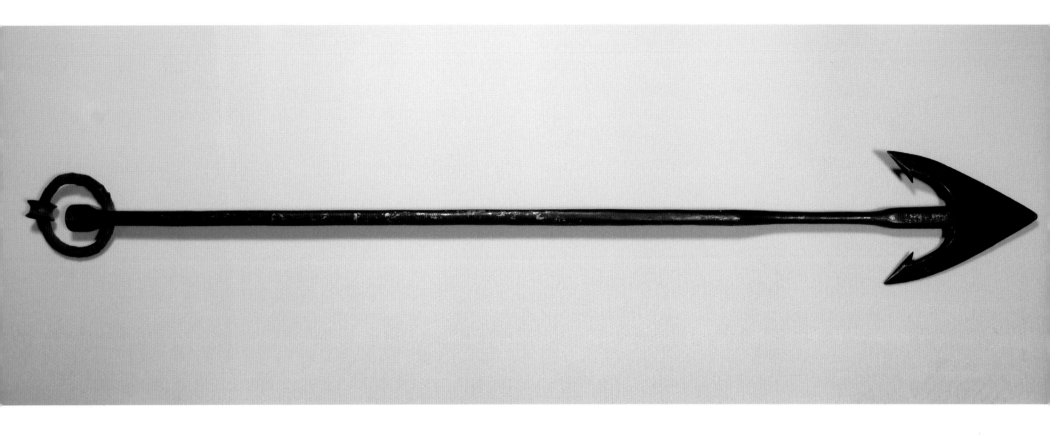

This is a fine example of a gun harpoon. A gun harpoon was one that was fired from a harpoon gun as opposed to a harpoon that was thrown by a man standing in the bows of a whaleboat. The shape of the head can clearly be seen, with the barbs to prevent it from sliding out of the whale once attached, and the 'stop withers' or counter barbs to ensure the barbs stayed in place. The moveable ring at the opposite side from the head was to connect the harpoon to a whaling line.

The harpoon is stamped 'J. L. P. 1884' and 'P. Star', which may indicate it was used on the whaling ship *Polar Star*. This vessel operated from Dundee from 1882 until 1899, when she was wrecked in Hudson Straits. There are persistent legends that this harpoon was used to hunt the famous Tay Whale in 1883, which would mean it was part of one of the most interesting stories to come out of the Firth of Tay. There was a John Paterson in the crew of *Polar Star* in 1889, and it would be fascinating, but perhaps too much of a coincidence, to think that it could be the same man who owned the harpoon.

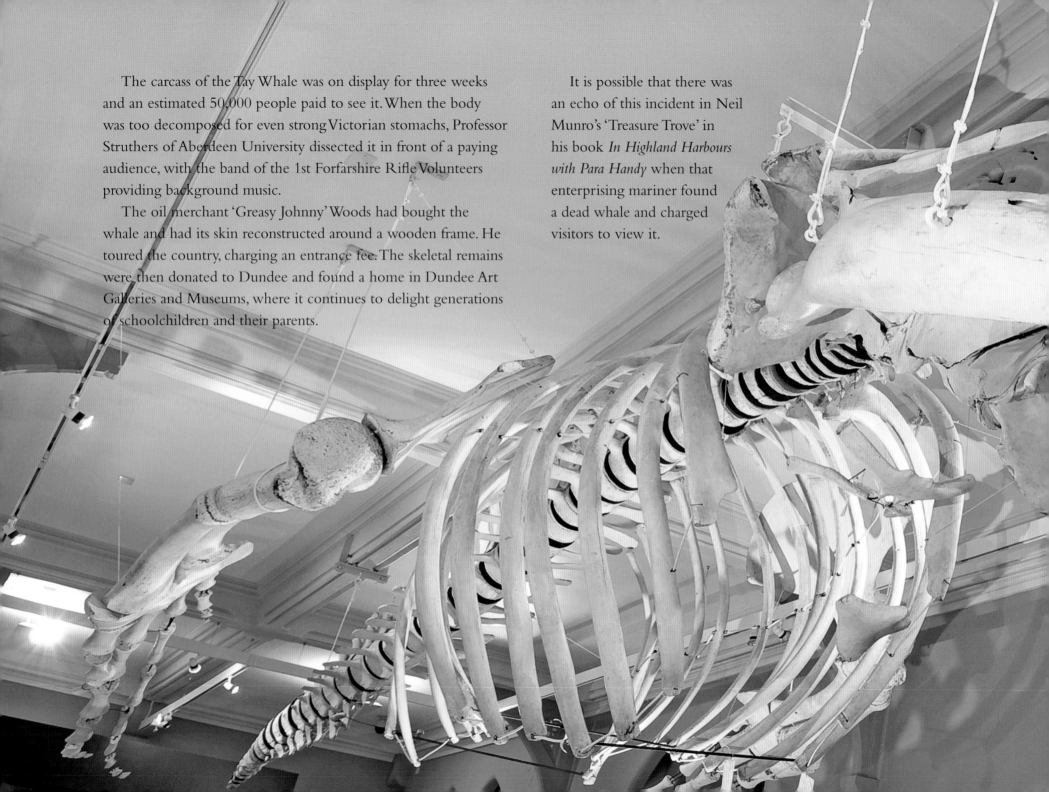

The carcass of the Tay Whale was on display for three weeks and an estimated 50,000 people paid to see it. When the body was too decomposed for even strong Victorian stomachs, Professor Struthers of Aberdeen University dissected it in front of a paying audience, with the band of the 1st Forfarshire Rifle Volunteers providing background music.

The oil merchant 'Greasy Johnny' Woods had bought the whale and had its skin reconstructed around a wooden frame. He toured the country, charging an entrance fee. The skeletal remains were then donated to Dundee and found a home in Dundee Art Galleries and Museums, where it continues to delight generations of schoolchildren and their parents.

It is possible that there was an echo of this incident in Neil Munro's 'Treasure Trove' in his book *In Highland Harbours with Para Handy* when that enterprising mariner found a dead whale and charged visitors to view it.

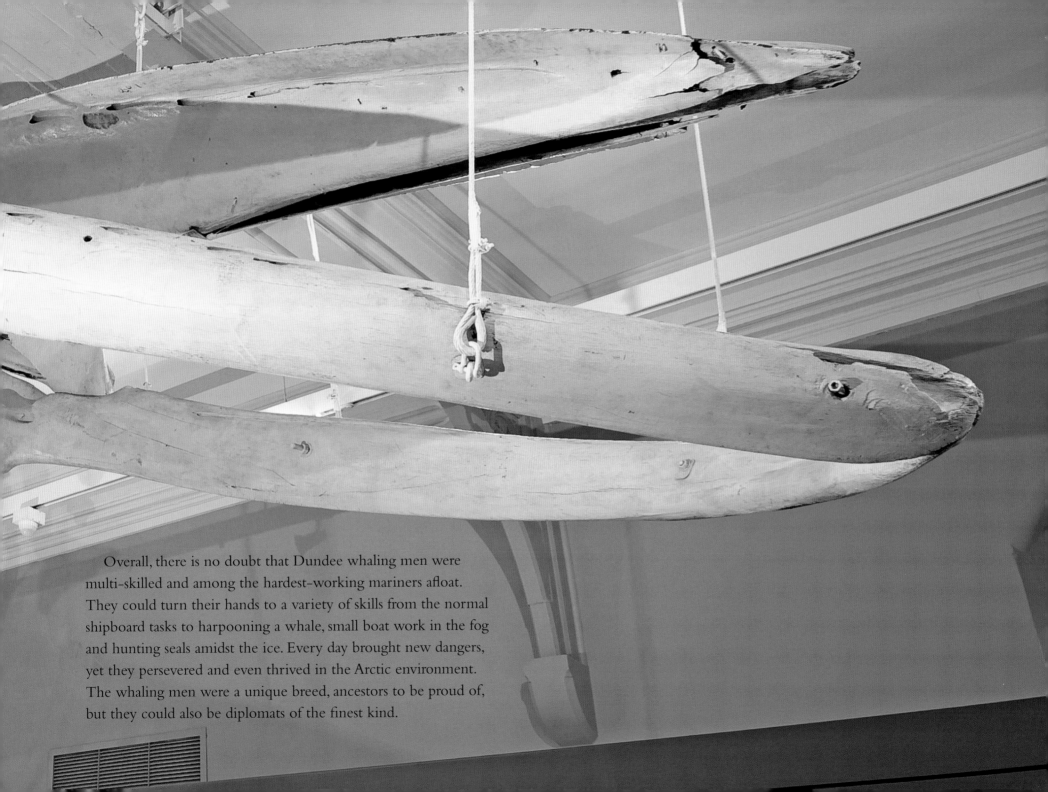

Overall, there is no doubt that Dundee whaling men were multi-skilled and among the hardest-working mariners afloat. They could turn their hands to a variety of skills from the normal shipboard tasks to harpooning a whale, small boat work in the fog and hunting seals amidst the ice. Every day brought new dangers, yet they persevered and even thrived in the Arctic environment. The whaling men were a unique breed, ancestors to be proud of, but they could also be diplomats of the finest kind.

DUNDEE WHALING MEN AND THE INUIT

The nineteenth century was a time of amazing expansion and discovery. Explorers pushed forward the boundaries of knowledge in every continent outside of Europe. There was also increased interest in the science of ethnology, the characteristics of different peoples.

Explorers and particularly scientists liked to study the various different and supposedly exotic peoples they met on their travels. Anybody who was not considered as mainstream was grist to the ethnographic mill, from Glasgow slum-dwellers to Pacific islanders. Arctic explorers were no different, so the Inuit people found themselves under scrutiny and cameras clicked to capture images

that were frozen in perpetuity. The photographers may have been thought intrusive at the time, but their work has helped preserve images of a culture that has all but gone now. It is sobering to consider that the continued presence of the whaling ships may have helped erode the culture that was captured in these pictures.

Dundee is fortunate that the Dundee Art Galleries and Museums hold an extensive selection of images of the Inuit, taken by various photographers who travelled on whaling ships. The Inuit are seen at home and on board the whaling ships, men, women and children mingling happily with each other as well as with the whaling men. This section shows a number of these

contact and exchanged ideas, goods and techniques.

This lantern slide shows a group of Inuit boarding *Eclipse*, an auxiliary steamer of the Dundee whaling fleet. The Inuit are boarding by means of a ladder that descends from her starboard bow to the ice. The crowd standing in the bow of *Eclipse* are ready to welcome them on board and show the friendship that developed between the men of the Dundee whaling fleet and the Inuit. From 1893 to 1908 Captain Milne was the master of *Eclipse*. In February 1897 the Dundee *Advertiser* claimed that his knowledge of Inuit life 'on the shores of Davis Strait is said to be more intimate than that of any other living European'. Given that he was a regular visitor to the Arctic from the age of seventeen and made an estimated forty-two voyages north, such an accolade is not surprising.

As well as being an expert on the Inuit, Captain Milne was an innovative whaling master. One of his suggestions was that when approaching a whale, his men should use paddles in the Inuit fashion, rather than oars. Paddles were quieter.

In the nineteenth century Dundee whaling vessels were frequent visitors to Arctic Canada and Greenland. The Dundee seamen fostered some very close links with the indigenous Inuit as the two peoples mingled together. Whaling men frequently mentioned the Inuit in their journals and logs. For example, in the journal he kept when he sailed in *Diana* in 1903, Alexander Lamb wrote, 'Some of the natives came aboard at night with barter. They were all very much amused at a phonograph.' Later in the same log Lamb noted, 'Some of the native women are good dancers.' Margaret Penny, one of the few whaling wives who sailed with her husband, 'found them [the Inuit] dancing reels with the greatest spirit'.

images, which demonstrate not only the link between Dundee whalers and the Inuit, but also show how wide the Dundee Art Galleries and Museums' range of images is to possibly stimulate further interest in this part of the collection.

As the whaling ships penetrated further north in their pursuit of whales, they came into contact with the native peoples of the Arctic. The whaling men and the Inuit established very friendly

Sometimes the relationships between whaling men and Inuit women progressed beyond barter and dancing. In 1885 the ship *Esquimaux* overwintered in Hudson's Bay and some whaling men brought Inuit women aboard for the season. The inevitable outcome of such close liaisons was a number of children with Dundee fathers and Inuit mothers. It says a great deal for the humanity of the Inuit that the children were adopted into their community with no fuss and total acceptance. The term political correctness had not been thought of in the whaling period, but the Inuit of the Arctic were natural practitioners of the art.

Dundee whaling seamen and the Inuit of Greenland and Eastern Canada were usually on the best of terms. The Inuit proved consistently hospitable whenever the Dundee men arrived. They taught the Dundee men Arctic techniques and helped guide them on the ice.

In return the Dundee men brought the Inuit onto the whaling ships. The Inuit had happy memories of the Scottish whalers. In her book *When the Whalers Were Up North: Inuit Memories from the Eastern Arctic*, Dorothy Eber quotes an elderly Inuit named Nutaraq who said, 'When ships came. . . my grandmother used to say, "If they ask you to dance for them, dance so they'll like you." . . . On one ship there was a man who would tease and make fun and chase me round the deck. . . this man who was so kind to me must have had children of his own.' Another Inuit woman named Anirnik said the Inuit children 'used to have "pretend" fathers' from the whalers and 'when we were getting on and off the ship we received presents from the white man'.

This print shows a group of Dundee whaling men and Inuit on the deck of a ship. The seaman on the extreme right at the back is holding an Inuit child with every appearance of affection.

In the year 1900 Francis Gillies, the Broughty Ferry photographer, signed on as a crewman on the Dundee whaling ship *Diana*. On his voyage to the Davis Strait he took some fascinating photographs, including this image of Inuit girls.

The photograph was taken at the Danish settlement at Godhavn (the Good Port – modern Qeqertarsuaq) on the island of Disko, on the west coast of Greenland. The dress of the girls is an indication of the attitudes of the period, when Europeans believed they had the right and the duty to impose their own ideas of civilisation on the indigenous peoples of whatever land they graced with their presence. In 1733 the Moravians were first to try to bring Christianity to Greenland; they remained a substantial presence until 1900, when the Danish National Church took over.

In 1773 the Danish government established the colony of Godhavn in an attempt to enforce Danish rights over the local whaling grounds. However, Dutch, German and British ships had already slaughtered huge numbers. From that date the Danes had a permanent presence in the settlement they made the capital of Northern Greenland. Many Dundee whaling ships called at Disko, searching for whales, replenishing stores or just to use the safe anchorage as a rendezvous.

Many people may imagine that the Inuit lived all their lives in igloos. However, the Arctic has summer as well as winter, and many Inuit lived semi-nomadic lives. It was normal for them to move three or four times in a year, visiting seasonal hunting grounds. In the winter they would live in igloos and hunt seals, but when spring came and the ice melted they moved to the coast, still catching seals and also fish. In the short summer they might head inland to hunt caribou, while always harvesting whatever food nature provided. They were very much hunter-gatherers with a routine that depended on the seasons and nature.

The arrival of the whaling men altered the traditional Inuit lifestyle by bringing them new tools, including firearms. In return the Inuit may have introduced whaling men to the art of scrimshaw as well as to Arctic survival, kayaks and hunting techniques. The pace of Inuit life altered completely during and after the Second World War. However, old photographs, such as those featured in this book, keep the memories of a near vanished culture alive.

This photograph shows the interior of a traditional Inuit summer tent. The front flap is open and the household goods can be clearly seen.

The Inuit had their own unique traditions and culture. Living in the Arctic, they developed a way of life that was perfect for their harsh environment. The Inuit were masters of their environment, able to adapt to life on the ice, on the water and in the tundra. They utilised everything that nature provided, to make themselves as comfortable as they could.

Although the Inuit kayak is very familiar today, their other vessel, the *omiack* or *umiack*, is less well known. This vessel was constructed of a frame of baleen or driftwood tied together and covered in sealskins. They were used in the summer to transport the people to the next hunting grounds, or sometimes to hunt walruses or even whales. Men used paddles when they travelled by *umiack*, but women used oars – although occasionally both genders might use sails. That style of craft was common to all the peoples who lived from Greenland to Siberia. A similar method of construction was used for the *curraghs* and *coracles* of Celtic Ireland and Scotland, proving that the cultures of indigenous peoples many thousands of miles apart can be very similar.

The *umiack* in this lantern slide holds sixteen people, many of them children. The photograph was taken from the deck of a Dundee whaling ship off the coast of Greenland.

This image shows two Inuit on the deck of a Dundee whaling ship. The photograph was taken by the explorer Sandon Perkins, and the Inuit are Etah natives from Greenland. They are eating raw seal fins, but are possibly deliberately posing for the camera, as both men are looking towards the lens. At this period of history there was a great interest in ethnography and the behaviour of people from other cultures fascinated the people in Britain. Perkins was only one of many photographers who took a trip to the more supposedly 'exotic' parts of the world to take photographs and collect information. Etah was a settlement near Reindeer Point in north-west Greenland. It was on the migration route from the Canadian Arctic to Greenland; the last such migration of Canadian Inuit was in 1865.

The picture shows how the deck of a whaling ship was used for different things, with a blacksmith's anvil behind the Inuit. This picture was taken in the Arctic, but the crewman at the back is wearing clothes that would not be out of place in Dundee, which suggests it was high summer. The Inuit are wearing their traditional clothes of leather jacket and fur trousers. The jacket could be seal leather and the trousers polar bear fur. Dundee imported sealskins for the city's own leather industry.

It was fairly common for whaling men to bring Inuit back with them to visit Scotland. One of them was named Schedule or Shoodlue, a medicine man who came to Dundee on *Eclipse* with Captain William Milne in 1894. Shoodlue had known the Dundee whaling men for years and was a particular friend of Captain Milne. He had approached *Eclipse* in his kayak off Cape York and had asked to be taken to Scotland. He spoke English well and helped out on the ship during the voyage. On arrival in Earl Grey Dock, several people came to visit him.

Shoodlue was an immediate hit with the people of Dundee and the surrounding area. Crowds gathered to greet him when he visited Broughty Ferry and, in November, Tayport. Shoodlue took part in temperance meetings and on two occasions he demonstrated his skill with the kayak in the Tay off the Esplanade.

He lived in the Sailor's Home in Dundee and was even more popular when he wore his native dress. The picture shows him dressed in furs and kneeling with a bow and arrow held in his left hand. When he travelled back home on *Eclipse* in 1895 the people of Dundee had given him so many gifts a whaleboat had to make two passages to carry them all.

Overall, the whaling men of Dundee and the Inuit achieved something rare in the nineteenth century. Men and women from vastly different cultures met and merged with friendship and mutual trust. The Inuit of Greenland and the Canadian Arctic proved hospitable hosts and in return the people of Dundee welcomed Inuit visitors into their city. As an example of a cross-cultural exchange, Inuit-Dundonian relations would be hard to beat.

FAREWELL TO AN ERA

Whaling, then, was a dirty, dangerous, raucous business that Dundee mariners and shipowners were involved in for over 160 years.

There were over a hundred Dundee vessels involved in that time, and each ship had its own unique history, but each slotted into the general pattern of the industry. There were years of profit and celebration that saw money rattle into the tills of the Dundee pubs, and years of mourning when tears filled the eyes of newly made widows. But after even the worst disasters, the mariners of Dundee picked themselves up, dusted themselves down and ventured north to brave the storms and savage ice of the North,

until there was neither profit nor point in their bravery.

After all that, after the last whaling ship left the docks and the last ton of blubber was boiled, after the last whaling mariner picked up his wages from behind the brass barrier in the office in Whale Lane and the last piece of baleen was exported overseas, what impact did whaling have on Dundee? Quite a lot. Whaling had created employment for thousands of Dundonians over a long period of time. Whaling had directly contributed to the jute industry that had made Dundee the leading jute city in the world and had given her the name of 'Juteopolis'. Whaling had directly contributed to the shipbuilding industry that had employed thousands and had produced some of the finest Arctic vessels the world had ever seen. Whaling had indirectly contributed to Dundee's leather industry while supplying the whaling vessels, and had involved farmers and grocers, rope makers and sail makers, blacksmiths, engineers and brewers. It had brought money to the town and occasionally a tinge of adventure to counterbalance the tragedy and heartache and constant worry. Whaling had been a way of life for thousands of mariners and their wives and families; the sight of a whaling ship leaving or entering the port had been a highlight in an often drab industrial existence, and the industry had contributed objects to the museum and university of the city.

Dundee had been an anomaly. The town had been involved in Arctic whaling from the early years of the 1750s and was the last British port to actively pursue the trade. Dundee had been innovative in its techniques, with steam vessels to push through the ice, men and ships overwintering in the Arctic, and bases in St John's. Dundee had been adaptable enough to use the advice of the Inuit and utilise the skills of the Newfoundlanders, hardy enough to venture into new whaling grounds in the Arctic and Antarctic and to hunt for new commodities. Most other towns had departed from whaling after the bad years of the 1830s and the advent of coal gas, and then petroleum drastically reduced the market for whale oil.

A fortunate combination of circumstances prolonged the industry in Dundee. There was the long-standing whaling industry with generations of experienced men; there was an established shipbuilding industry; there were hundreds of mariners and a good harbour; there was a class of entrepreneurs who were not afraid to put their money into whaling; and lastly there was the burgeoning jute industry that required tons of whale oil every year. Yet in the end even Dundee had been forced to call it quits and withdraw from their Arctic adventure.

For all the 160-odd years and the thousands of men, there is little remaining to remind people that Dundee was once the leading Arctic whaling port in Europe. Where Whale Lane stood there is now a car park and a swimming pool; the shipbuilding yards have been built over, but fading echoes of the past remain in Mary Ann Lane that was once the whale-oil boiling yards for the Mary Ann Whale Fishing Company; and the ghosts of the old whaling men remain in the Arctic Bar, where, according to legend, they were once paid. There is also the image collection in Dundee Art Galleries and Museums.

In the over 160 years of Dundee's involvement with Arctic whaling there were an estimated 110 ships associated with the industry sailing from the port. With an average of forty seamen on every ship and an estimated average of five ships a year sailing from Dundee that would give around 200 whaling seamen every year. If only 40 per cent of these men came from Dundee, there would be around 22,000 seamen voyages. Some men made whaling their life and embarked on forty or so voyages; others found that one Arctic voyage was more than enough. If we take five voyages as a very rough average, then there would have been 4,400 Dundee seamen involved in the whaling industry – that is a very conservative estimate. The images in this book will allow the descendants of these men the opportunity to see the kind of lives their ancestors had when they worked and lived in the Arctic.

BIBLIOGRAPHY

From Dundee Art Galleries and Museums

Campbell, Matthew. *Diary of a Voyage to the Davis Strait Aboard the* Nova Zembla *of Dundee 1884 by Matthew Campbell, Surgeon*. 1884.

Cargo Book of Dorothy. 1832.

Davidson, Captain Thomas. *Journal of a Voyage from Dundee Towards the Davis Strait On Board the* Dorothy *in 1834*. 4 June 1834.

Kinnes Journal

Wanless, John. *Journal of a Voyage to Baffin Bay Aboard the Ship* Thomas *Commanded by Alex Cooke*. 1834.

Whaling Log of Alexander J. Lamb.

From Local History Department, Central Library Dundee

Dundee Directories. [various dates]

Ingram, John P. *Papers Whaling and Sealing*.

Ingram, John P. *Shipping Information A-D D31111*.

Lamb Collection: *Whaling*.

Ledger of the Tay Whaling Company 1815–1821.

Smith, Alexander. *An Account of a Voyage to Greenland Aboard the Whaler SS* Camperdown *in the Year 1861, written and illustrated by Alexander Smith of Dundee, chief engineer*. 1861.

From Dundee City Archives

Customs and Excise Records.

Dundee Register of Shipping.

Dundee Year Book. [various dates]

From Dundee University Archive Services

MS 57/3/2: Dorothy Whale Fishing Company Accounts.

MS 254: David Henderson Collection.

MS 254/2/1/13: *Voyage to Davis Straits by Thomas Macklin on board the SS* Narwhal.

MS 254/2/1/16: *Vannet Logs*.

MS 254/2/1/18 Walker, A. Barclay. *The Cruise of the* Esquimaux *(steam whaler) to Davis Straits and Baffin Bay April to October 1899*. Liverpool: 1909.

University of St Andrews Special Collection

University of St Andrews Special Collection MS 15914

Newspapers

Aberdeen Journal

Caledonian Mercury

Dundee Advertiser

Dundee Courier

Primary Sources

Barron, William. *Old Whaling Days*. Hull: 1895.

Bruce, William. *S. Polar Exploration*. London: 1911.

Burn Murdoch, W. G. *From Edinburgh to the Antarctic*. London: 1894.

Dobson, David. *Scottish Whalers Before 1800* (n.d.). St Andrews. *Extracts from the Records of the Convention of the Royal Burghs of Scotland*, Volume 4. Edinburgh: 1917.

MacLeod, Innes (ed.). *To the Greenland Sea: Alexander Trotter's Journal of the Voyage of the Enterprise in 1856 from Fraserburgh and Lerwick*. Lerwick: 1979.

Markham, Captain A. H. *A Whaling Cruise to Baffin's Bay and the Gulf of Boothia and an Account of the Rescue of the Crew of the Polaris*. London: 1874.

Mawson, Douglas. *The Home of the Blizzard*. London & Kent Town: 1915, 1996.

Starke, June (transcriber). *Baffin Fair: Experiences of George Laing, a Scottish Surgeon in the Arctic Whaling Fleet 1830 and 1831*. Hull: 2003.

Secondary Sources

Archibald, Malcolm. *Whalehunters: Dundee and the Arctic Whalers*. Edinburgh: 2004.

Clark, Captain G. *The Last of the Whaling Captains*. Glasgow: 1986.

Dyson, John. *The Hot Arctic*. London: 1979.

Francis, Daniel. *Arctic Chase: A History of Whaling in Canada's North*. St John's: 1984.

Henderson, David S. *Fishing for the Whale: A Guide/Catalogue to the Collection of Whaling Relics in Dundee Museums*. Dundee: 1976.

Jackson, Gordon. *Research in Maritime History, No 29: The British Whaling Trade*. St John's: 2006.

Lubbock, Basil. *The Arctic Whalers*. Glasgow: 1937, 1955.

Sanger, C. W. 'The Dundee–St John's Connection: Nineteenth-Century Interlinkages Between Scottish Arctic Whaling and the Newfoundland Seal Fishery.' *Newfoundland Studies*, 4.1. St John's Newfoundland: 1988.

Sanger, C. W. *The Origins of the Scottish Northern Whale Fishery*. Unpublished PhD Thesis, University of Dundee: 1985.

Whatley, Christopher A., David B. Swinfen, and Annette M., Smith. *The Life and Times of Dundee*. Edinburgh: 1993.

GLOSSARY OF WHALING TERMS

a fall: A successful strike by a harpooner

articles: Contract signed by crew members before beginning of voyage

baleen: Also known as whalebone: the plates of horn-like material used by some species of whale to filter plankton from the sea. The plates are suspended from the whale's upper jaws. This was one of the main materials sought by whaling men

barque: Sailing vessel of three masts, with square-rigged sails on the fore and main masts and fore and aft sails on the mizzen

blubber: The layer of fat beneath a whale's skin. This material was brought back to port and boiled to make the very valuable whale oil

blubber boat: Whaling ship

carvel built: A wooden-built vessel where the planks of the hull are laid edge-to-edge to have a smooth finish; this was the more usual type of hull for whaling ships

clinker built: Wooden ship where the lower edge of one side plank overlaps the upper edge of the one below

crow's nest: Sometimes known as the 'barrel'. This was an enclosed, barrel-shaped lookout position that was hoisted up the main mast in the whale-hunting areas. It could have a seat and be equipped with a telescope; sometimes it was lined with straw. Scoresby the Whitby whaler is sometimes credited with its invention, but the Americans also claim to have invented it

doubled: A hull with double the thickness of planking to make it stronger in the ice

fast boat: A boat attached 'fast' to the whale by a harpoon and line

fish: Whaling term for the whale

flensing: The process of stripping blubber from the carcass of a whale

floe: A sheet of ice

flukes: The tail of a whale

foreganger: The length of line, about three fathoms (eighteen feet), attached to the harpoon at one end and to the whale line proper at the other. It 'gangs before' the line

Greener gun: For firing harpoon into whales. This weapon had a two-inch bore (the width of the barrel) and was mounted in the bows of whaling boats. Although the first was invented as early as 1733, they were not commonly used until the 1790s, when percussion caps replaced the old flintlock mechanism. However, many whaling vessels used hand-thrown harpoons well into the nineteenth century

Greenman: Or first voyager: a seaman who is on his first voyage in a whaling vessel. In order to qualify for the whaling bounty (1733–1824), whaling ships had to carry a specified number of Greenmen

loose harpooner: Harpooner on trial or without a fixed position in the ship

lowery tow: The length of cable used for securing the skins of dead seals as they were dragged over the ice

making off: The process of cutting blubber into small pieces for stowing in casks below deck

nipped: Crushed between two floes of ice

pan: A pile of dead seals

schooner: A vessel rigged with fore and aft sails. She has two or more masts; if she has square topsails on her foremast she would be a topsail schooner

screw: Or propeller: the rotating device that drives a ship through the water

scrimshaw: The traditional art of the whaling man, usually a design picked out on a piece of baleen, a sperm whale tooth or a piece of walrus ivory. It was also known as 'bone carving'

ship: In the days of sail, a ship was a vessel with three masts or more

specktioneer or spectioneer: The head harpooner or officer in charge of removing the blubber from the whale

sweiler: Sealing seaman from Newfoundland

uni or unicorn: Narwhal

whaleboat or whaler: An open boat, normally, but not always, sharp at both ends. A whaling boat had a crew of six men but no rudder – it was manoeuvred with a long steering oar. Livvies was the main Dundee firm that made these vessels

white whale: Narwhal or beluga